WISDOM OF DREAMING

A GUIDE TO AN
EFFECTIVE DREAM LIFE

WISDOM OF DREAMING

A GUIDE TO AN
EFFECTIVE DREAM LIFE

PAUL M. SHELDON, M.A.

Limnosophy Publishing
Ashland, Oregon

Wisdom of Dreaming: A Guide to an Effective Dream Life

Copyright © 2017 Paul M. Sheldon, M.A.
www.limnosophy.net

First published in the United States of America in 2017 by Limnosophy, LLC.

Cover owl, back cover, and layout design by Eduardo Lista Oleynick
Set by Eduardo Lista Oleynick

Printed in the United States of America.

This publication is designed to provide accurate and authoritative information about the wisdom of dreaming.

It is sold under the express understanding that any decisions or actions you take as a result of reading this book must be based on your personal and professional judgement and will be at your sole discretion and your sole risk. The author will not be held responsible for the consequences of any actions and/or decisions made as a result of any information given or recommendations made herein.

This publication is designed to provide accurate and authoritative information with regard to the subject manner covered. It is sold with the understanding that the publisher is not engaged in rendering legal, accounting, or other professional advice. If legal advice or other expert assistance is required, the services of a competent professional person should be sought. --From a Declaration of Principles jointly adopted by a Committee of the American Bar Association and a Committee of Publishers and Associations.

Cataloguing-in-Publication Data

Sheldon, Paul
    Wisdom of Dreaming: A Guide to an Effective Dream Life
    ISBN 978-0-692-91260-7 1. Dreams I. Title
    154.6'3--dc22

First printing July 2017
ISBN 978-0-692-91260-7

This book is available at quantity discounts for bulk purchases. For information, contact the publisher at limnosophy@gmail.com.

Dedicated to creative dreamers.

TABLE OF CONTENTS

PREFACE

Enjoying and realizing dreams has been my favorite fascination, for more than 60 years. I have always been blessed with abundant dream recall and have also always loved the process by which dreams move from fantasy to reality in waking life. A youthful era of dancing, singing, and exploring various aspects of consciousness and spiritual experience flowed smoothly into an adulthood of consulting and advising, helping other people realize their fondest dreams. In college, in the 1970s and '80s, I titled my master's thesis in human development at Pacific Oaks College, in Pasadena, California, *Dreams for the Future,* for which I studied creative dreamers, whose visions and dreams led to specific organizations and institutions serving millions of people through tree planting, traditional dance, performance art, and programs for children and their parents. Although I had always been interested in dreams as unique expressions of consciousness and opportunities for creative play and creative realization, in 1978, thanks to an article in Marilyn Ferguson's newsletter, *Brain/ Mind Bulletin*, I discovered Dr. Stephen LaBerge's work in "lucid dreaming." This led to decades of careful exploration of the possibilities of conscious dreaming — dreaming while knowing oneself as the dreamer — as well as extensive reading and study of everything I could find about dreaming, and everything I could find about comparative religions and varieties of religious and spiritual experience, all of which eventually led to this book — *Dreamosophy.* I sincerely hope you find the ideas, opportunities, and exercises in this book useful, and that you also find *Dreamosophy* and the world of dreaming to be a portal through which you can pass into a realm of realizing *your* fondest dreams!

—Paul Sheldon, Ashland, Oregon, May 2017.

ACKNOWLEDGEMENTS

After 50 years of research, it's difficult to thank everyone! Dr. Jack Rains' 1970 college course in Existential Phenomenological Psychology at Duquesne University took me from math egghead to student of consciousness. The wonderful master's degree program in human development, at Pacific Oaks College, in Pasadena, California, provided marvelous support to explore human awareness, consciousness, mythology, dreams, metaphors, group processes, human biology, sexuality, anthropology, sociology, existential phenomenology, and a much wider range of study than more "traditional" programs, all of which eventually led to this book, beginning as my master's thesis, *Dreams for the Future*. My dance mentors and literally hundreds of thousands of others kept my spirit alive and thriving, through the miracle of the Sacred Circle of the Dance – truly a dream come true! I especially want to thank Rudy Dannes, Athan Karras, Chalo Holguin, Dick Oakes, Rubi Vuceta, David Shochat, Steve Murillo, Caroline Cox Barns, Karen Doring Boggs, Paul Gale, Stewart Mennin, Tzigane McDonough, Julie Bracker, Louise Bilman, Tom Bozigian, Dennis Boxell, Mihai and Alexandru David, Dick Crum, Israel Yakovee, Dani Dassa, George Nichols, Nikos Savvidis, Barry Glass, Dayle Ulbricht, Dana Matchette, Jordan Cole, Dana Fielding, Don Sparks, Billy Burke, Miguel Tejada-Flores, Frank Tripi, Dori Aloni Meshi, David Katz, Judy Purdy Eden, Niko Culevski, Anthony Shay, Mario Casillas, Roz Witt, Madeline Taylor, Pearl Rottenberg, Peter and Trudy Israel, Don Green & Barbara Weismann, Vince and Robin Evanchuk, Linnea Mandell, Craig Kurumada, Greg & Becky Deja, Jasna Pecaric, David Katz, Dori Aloni Meshi, Don Green and his little brother Bob, my older sister, L. Hunter Lovins, and my wife and favorite dance friend, Anne Sheldon, all of whom have been the very best friends any dreamer could ever hope for. Of course, very special thanks are due to my amazingly tolerant and supportive parents, Dr. Ethel Farley Hunter Sheldon and Dr. Paul M. Sheldon, Sr., and to my older siblings, L. Hunter Lovins, Willliamson Whitehead Fuller, III, Edith Fuller, and Carlo Sheldon, who almost always believed, encouraged, supported, and allowed me to live life to the fullest, as a dream come true. I shall always, always feel the deepest gratitude. The contributions of Dr. Stephen LaBerge's work on lucid dreaming to the development of *Dreamosophy* cannot be underestimated, along with the friendship and support of Jennifer Dole and Michael and Pamela LaPointe. My fundamental grounding in the experience of dreaming emerged from many dream experiences inspired by Dr. LaBerge's books, *Lucid Dreaming* and *Exploring the World of Lucid Dreaming*, as well as our work together at the Lucidity Institute, in 1991. Similarly, the book *Creative Dreaming*, by Dr. Patricia Garfield and Alan McGlashan's *The Savage and Beautiful Country*, as well as Dorothy Bryant's *The Kin of Ata Are Waiting For You* and Ursula LeGuin's *The Lathe of Heaven* preceded the lucid dreaming work in very significant ways, along with Charles Tart's work on discrete states of awareness. Reading and exploring Dr. Richard Corriere and Dr. Joseph Hart's book *The Dream Makers*, as well as my subsequent friendship with Richard Corriere formed the basis for most of the exercises and activities contained in this book. I am deeply indebted to Dr. Corriere, for his friendship and permission to develop the exercises from the book *The Dream Makers*, first published by Drs. Corriere and Hart in L.A., in book form, in 1977; and subsequently as a series of pamphlets, by me, in Aspen, Colorado, in 1983, and later as a series of online webinars, in 2011-2013, with help from Diane Dandeneau and George Kao. In Aspen, the support and encouragement of my dear friend and Tai Chi Teacher, Marcia Corbin and my former wife, Janet Frosh Newman, also were pivotal to the development of what eventually came to be known as *Dreamosophy*, as was the wonderful art of my dear friend and world-renowned water color artist, Lee Shapiro. Many happy times with John Denver and Tom Crum at Windstar were yet another dream come true. Tara Miller and Sam Brown also believed in and encouraged me during the Aspen years and throughout subsequent decades of friendship. Dr. Christine Perala Gardiner's guidance and support for my explorations into Stephan Hoeller's work and her deep understanding of the living gnosis and the practices of Christian Gnosticism, as well as her equally-deep understanding of the importance of intact watersheds, sacred groves, and sacred dances as embodiments of Divine Presence, also contributed profoundly to the development of the *Dreamosophy* approach. Laura X, a truly altruistic catalyst for positive change has been and continues to be a stalwart friend and role model. Laura X's dream of a world in which dignity and respect for all replace "rape culture" and violence of all kinds, especially violence and abuse towards women, continues to inspire me as one of the most profoundly meaningful and relevant dreams of human history — Laura, may all your fondest dreams come true, for the good of all! Similarly, the vision and work of my dear older sister, L. Hunter Lovins, provides one of the most lasting and hopeful dreams of all time — I hold similar aspirations for the realization of Hunter's dreams of a regenerative world culture. Martha Edwards and Bob Green welcomed me into their wonderful home in Creve Coeur, MO, many times, as *Dreamosophy* has evolved, offering words of encouragement, warm friendship, and highly capable website advice and assistance (plus wonderful music and dancing!). Thanks, also to Trevor Oliver, for advance help converting the early webinars to apps! John and Margo Steiner-King, Cody Oreck, Randy and Dan Compton, and all my friends in and around Boulder have also been continuously supportive! Particular thanks are due to Diane Dandeneau, artist, folk singer, song writer, web guru, and friend of God, whose Divine Mastery Course led to my receiving endorsement from the Divine Radiant Beings of Rainbow Love and Light to begin speaking publically about this material.

Thanks, Diane for our first website, www.limnosophy.net, and for helping get the first webinars out onto the Web! I also deeply appreciate the friendship and support of master marketer Tom Ruppanner; inspiring entrepreneur and author Marvin Klein, (Founder of Chicago's PortionPac Chemical Company); and master marketer Michael Griffin, of Zu-USA (Thank you, Michael, for first suggesting the word, "Dreamosophy"). These three, in particular, provided kind encouragement, support, and ideas to write a book — your gentle enthusiasm made the current volume possible. Likewise, Elizabeth Eagar's and Chelsey Thompson's gracious assistance as "ghost writers" in adapting the original pamphlets and online webinars into book form were swift and steady — Liz and Chelsey, I don't think this book would have happened without you! David Katz's, Lora Jo Foo's, Kari Sherman's, Roxane Schwabe's, and Christine Perala Gardiner's dedication to the first round of online webinars presenting the *Dreamosophy* materials, in 2012 and 2013, also made this book possible. My profound gratitude also goes to the Amazing Lauren Peckman, contra dance caller, dreamer, and accomplished biblical exegete; to Kari Sherman, dream teacher, tai chi instructor, and permaculturist; to Anthony Forrest, educator and entrepreneur; and to Alisia Brown, educator, youth advocate, and street canvasser par excellence; who have stepped forward to serve as the first Dreambassadors! And these few final words serve to express my sincere gratitude to the thousands of other supporters and dance partners, whose love and friendship made *Dreamosophy* possible. Thanks, thanks, and thanks again, one and all! Blessed Be!

INTRODUCTION

Becoming more open to your dreams can be one of the most rewarding experiences of your life. Sometime dreams are terrifying, but they don't have to stay that way. Deepening and expanding your relationship with your own dream life allows you to learn more about your daily life — aspects you want to explore and aspects you may not want to explore. While there are already some dynamic confluences between your dream life and your waking life, many people spend so much time analyzing their dreams or ignoring their dreams that they miss out on many of the benefits they can get from dreams and dreaming.

This guidebook outlines the Dreamosophy approach. Dreamosophy – literally, the wisdom of dreaming – approaches dreams and dreaming differently from other traditions. The Dreamosophy approach can help you to find confluences between dreaming and waking, and can help you make the changes you long for, to have your life become a dream come true. In this guidebook, you will learn many valuable ideas, to take those first steps toward a deeper and more satisfying dream life! Through the Dreamosophy approach, you can discover and co-create your own, inner wisdom – the wisdom of dreaming!

First, this guidebook will talk about some of the steps that you can take to remember your dreams. It starts out with some of the common myths that come with dreaming and why these myths are holding you back from your true potential as a creative dreamer. After understanding these myths, you will be invited to move on to some of the simple steps that you can take to start remembering more dreams. It is impossible to continue to some of the other steps in this guidebook if you find it hard to remember your dreams, so the first section of this guidebook will focus on this important first step of remembering your dreams.

The following chapters will focus on the Dream Opportunities, which are a major component of the Dreamosophy approach. In these chapters, you will learn how to be free in your dreams, how to feel good in your dreams, how to speak up in your dreams, how to make friends in your dreams, and finally how to understand and realize your dreams. Each chapter is divided into three levels that help you gradually reach the full potential of each Dream Opportunity. These three levels include noticing, identifying, and transforming. As you explore your way through each level, you can develop the skills needed to help you progress and experience success as a creative dreamer.

Finally, this guidebook concludes with information on how to become a Dreambassador, so you can help others to reach their full potential as creative dreamers, too.

Understanding your dreams and how they work can make a big difference in your life, but it doesn't need to be as complicated as others may have led you to believe. As you follow the tips in this guidebook and learn about the Dreamosophy approach, it can be easy to unlock your true potential, with the help of your dreams.

1: HOW TO REMEMBER YOUR DREAMS

Remembering your dreams can be a wonderful experience. You can enjoy and learn from each dream's story when you are sleeping – you can make new friends, speak up in your dreams, and do so much more. Most of us fall asleep at night and wake up the next morning having no idea what happened the night before. This can be a huge missed opportunity. Remembering your dreams doesn't have to be challenging, but it does require a bit of attention and dedication from you. The payoff is worth it, especially when you can get so much more out of your sleep than just rest.

Before you can follow any of the other steps that are outlined in this guidebook, you must be able to remember some of your dreams. In the beginning, you may find that you remember just a few dreams here and there, and that is a good start; but with some of the suggestions in this chapter, you may start to have more vivid dreams – dreams that you can remember better than before. This makes the process easier.

Each step in this book asks you to remember your dreams. Sometimes, you can make up a dream or recall one from the past to help complete the exercises in this guidebook, but the best way to make these steps work is to remember your most recent dream and then accept that one as the most important dream to attend to right now. This chapter helps you to get started with remembering your dreams so that the other steps are easier to explore later!

COMMON MYTHS ABOUT DREAMS

Remembering your dreams is a great gift. Dreams can tell a story, show some parallels between your waking life and your dreams, and they can even help you feel good. It does take some practice to learn how to remember your dreams, but being purposeful in your approach and actively trying to remember your dreams often make a big difference and can help you to bring those dreams out of the shadows.

Before we get into the basics of remembering your dreams, let's address some of the simple myths that are often in the background, when we consider dreams. These myths can hold you back and can make it harder to remember your dreams. Sometimes, these myths even downplay the importance of remembering your dreams, and make you miss out. Some myths that you can watch out for include:

Myth #1: Dreams are just distractions or "day residue."

Many people assume that dreams are only distractions — simply thoughts and feelings that are left over from the day — not something important for you to enjoy or learn from. This myth assumes that dreams are not that important, because they just sort through the information from the day, repeating the things that you went through already. When you think about dreams in this way, you assume that they are not that important, and if you just ignore them, you won't miss out on anything.

The truth: Your dreams are merely a distraction, because you don't know how to pay careful attention to them. There are some great things that occur in your dreams, from meeting new people to learning lessons along the way. You can just learn how to pay attention and remember your dreams. These dreams are not just little snippets that can distract you when you are sleeping, but important experiences that you can learn from and grasp once you learn how.

You may find that, in some cases, there are connections between your dreams and your waking life. This is normal, and as you go through some of the different steps in this guidebook, you may find that this happens, more often than not. But this does not mean that dreams are just a distraction or that they are just some blank images of the day that you just finished. These connections are important. They can help you to experience what is going on with your feelings and your freedom, and you can use the dreams to help you improve your waking life.

If you have never explored your dreams, it is easy to believe that the images in your dreams are just random thoughts and ideas. But as you move through this guidebook, you may find that your dreams can have a purpose. When you intentionally look through your dreams, you are more likely to find some of the connections that exist between your waking life and your dream life.

Myth #2: You should try to control, change, or manipulate your dreams.

Another common myth that comes with dreaming is that you should try to control and manipulate your dreams. There is a growing school of thought that teaches people how they can be the one who controls these dreams and get the results that they want. But doesn't this just sound exhausting? Dreaming is supposed to be a time when you can relax and enjoy what is going on around you, not a time where you have to put in more work. Over time, "working" can lead you to feel exhausted or frustrated.

The truth: If you invest your sleep time trying to change, manipulate, or control the things that you are doing in your dreams, your dreaming can become hard work. Dreaming is a time to relax, to have fun, to learn, and to enjoy an experience like no other. If you are trying to change or control your dreams, you may just be distracting yourself from the enjoyment and learning that can happen naturally while dreaming.

It is not your job to try to control or change your dreams, but you can be deliberate and try to make some changes in the way that you approach your dreams during your waking life. Remember that your waking life and your dream life are connected, in more ways than you can imagine. So, if you are able to change the way you behave in your waking world (by being more attentive and more intentional about your dream life), you may start to see this in your dreams.

Myth #3: You must analyze your dreams.

Another myth that you may have heard is that if you want to get value out of your dreams, you have to spend a lot of time analyzing and interpreting your dreams. While there are some dreams that provide a lot of value to the dreamer, investing too much time analyzing each dream can just distract you along the way. Many people who try to interpret their dreams are just going to distract themselves rather than sitting back and enjoying learning from the dreams they have naturally. In addition, this over-analysis can add a lot of stress to the dreams when you worry about missing little details or when you worry about the big message that is supposed to be there.

The truth: When it comes to dreaming, if you try to understand, analyze, and interpret your dreams, you are just likely to distract yourself and you may miss out on some of the amazing things that can be found in your dreams naturally and spontaneously. In this guidebook, we invest some more time talking about how to remember your dreams. This will help you to get the most from your dreams. But, if you make it hard work, you may not be able to enjoy and learn from the dream situations you are in, in the same ways. You can just allow dreaming to be more natural, and then you may be able to truly enjoy and learn from the dreams you dream.

Dreaming is not all about the work. You may have been told for many years that you need to study your dreams, write them down, and then spend days analyzing what everything in each dream means. But the thought of this can make you feel exhausted. Many people may give up because of the work and the volume of information over time. As you will see, with the approach that is given in this guidebook, dreaming does not have to be a challenge or a lot of work. Just a few minutes each day is enough to help you to start deepening your dream life and having more enjoyable and beneficial dream experiences – dreams that work for you, not against you.

You may find that there are many more myths out there about dreams. People often come up with their own thought processes about dreams and it is not uncommon to find other courses and information that pertain to your dreams and how to make them work for you. But most of these techniques are not as useful, because they are based in the myths above and can be too hard or too distracting for you to work with. When you dispel some of these myths, you can focus on experiencing your dreams, without having to worry that you aren't spending enough time on it or analyzing your dreams enough.

The approach that is shown in this guidebook is easy to use. It doesn't require you to spend hours on your dreams nor do you need to become an expert in the field to make any sense of your dreams. Acting in this way simply makes you tired and can make dreaming a hard job. Dreaming is supposed to be relaxing, it is about feeling good about yourself and having some fun. Yes, it can be a reflection on your waking life, but you can use that to your advantage, rather than feeling obligated and pulled down from your dreams.

The techniques in this guidebook may help to make this possible, and you may be surprised by how easy it can be. You won't have to worry about doing it wrong or having a bad day, because you can just start again the next day, if needed. You can go at your own pace and the results will find you, as long as you dedicate a little time and attention to making it happen.

THE BASICS OF THE DREAMOSOPHY APPROACH

To get started on this guidebook, there are a few simple steps, which are separated into chapters. In addition to helping you remember dreams, this guidebook is all about making your dreams your own, rather than just being there. It's about being free, feeling good, speaking up, making friends, and understanding and realizing your dreams. Many people go to bed and have a dream without remembering it. In many instance, they are really missing out on some of the cool things, and some of the lessons and deeper experiences, that can come up in dreams. The five basic Dream Opportunities, which are discussed in more detail throughout each chapter of this guidebook, include:

- How to be free in your dreams
- How to feel good in your dreams
- How to speak up in your dreams
- How to make friends in your dreams
- How to understand and realize your dreams

Each of these chapters is important to helping you deepen and expand the value of your dreams. Of course, the first step is to remember your dreams. If you are not able to remember the dreams you are having, it can be very difficult to learn how to be free, feel good, speak up, or make friends in them. So, let's get started with some of the basics that may help you to remember your dreams!

As you go through this guidebook, you will learn about all the sections of the Dreamosophy approach. Each Dream Opportunity is divided into three parts – noticing, identifying, and transformation or change. All of these are important, because they help you deepen and expand your experience of your dreams in a manner that is steady, but slow enough not to cause too much strain for you.

In the first level, you are simply responsible for noticing things. For example, if you would prefer to feel good in your dreams, just monitor your dreams for a week and then write down how you feel in each of the dreams. By asking questions about how you feel, you can start to notice a few patterns. At this level, you are just noticing what goes on, and nothing else.

In the second level, you are invited to identify these same feelings in your waking life. Your dream life is going to have many connections to your waking life, so during this stage, you may want to invest time identifying the feelings that you have on most days and comparing them to your dream life. At this point, you still aren't taking any actions yet, just noticing the patterns.

Finally, in the third level, you will be invited to explore transformation. In this level, you will invest a few days considering what it would be like to shift some aspects of how you experience your daily life. If you are attending to feelings, you can invest this time considering your feelings for that day. When you feel happy, you will be invited to imagine what it would be like for those feelings to intensify and/or decrease any way you choose (as long as you don't harm yourself or anyone else). You can do the same with any of the feelings you have during that day.

You can do this with all five basic Dream Opportunities discussed in this guidebook. The aspiration here is to recognize patterns in your dream life and your waking life, and then consider what it would be like to make changes in your waking life. Many of these possibilities will also show up in your dream life, without having to work so hard while you are asleep. Your sleeping time should be relaxing; and while you are focusing on finding some of the patterns in your dreams, most of the exploration takes place while you are awake.

This guidebook goes into more depth about how these three levels work and what you can do with them based on the Dream Opportunity in each chapter. This is a gradual process that starts with you just noticing things in your dreams and ends with some potentially significant and important shifts in your waking life – shifts that can be deeply satisfying in creative ways.

GETTING STARTED

Now that you understand a little bit more about the Dreamosophy approach, you are cordially invited to move on to the first step. To make any of these steps work for you, it is important for you to learn how to remember some of your dreams. You can choose to make up a dream to help with some of the steps, but the most effective way to benefit from this guidebook is to remember your dreams when you first wake up.

Most people can remember some of their dreams on occasion, but remembering dreams on a regular basis can be a challenge. If you only remember a handful of your dreams each month, going through this approach can take a long time.

In this section, you will learn some great tips to start remembering your dreams, so you can move easily through the steps that are given later on.

Before you are able to begin remembering your dreams, you need to go to sleep! A good night's sleep is one of the best ways to have clear and vivid dreams that you may be able to remember the next day. If you have trouble falling asleep at night, if you have to get up a lot, or if you just aren't able to fall into a deep sleep when your head hits the pillow, you may find that it is really hard to remember your dreams. The good news is that there are a few simple things you can do to make sure that you get the right amount of sleep for your body, including:

• Drink enough water: Going to bed dehydrated sometimes keeps you from going into a deep sleep. You may be able to fall asleep, but in the back of your awareness maybe you are thirsty. Get enough water (not too much) and then make sure that you go to the bathroom before sleeping, so you can really fall asleep well and easily. You might consider keeping a glass of water by your bed, as well, to help you get a few sips of water if you do wake up feeling thirsty.
• Enjoy some time outside: Too many of us spend our time inside, working, watching television, doing chores, or getting other things done. If you want to be successful with getting to sleep at night, many people benefit from being exposed to "full-spectrum" light (also known as sunlight), which can only be found outside or in day-lit buildings with natural light. Consider investing at least an hour outside each day, to get the many benefits of natural sunlight.
• Eat a simple diet: Consider eating a diet that is simple, but full of natural, whole foods. Foods that are highly-processed, as well as stimulating and sweetened foods, can be bad for the body and may not be nutritionally complete. Stimulants like coffee, tea, caffeinated drinks, or mate may also make it difficult to fall asleep. Stick with foods that are whole and natural, such as fresh produce, so that the body can get the nutrients that it needs to stay healthy and you are able to fall asleep easily.
• Enjoy moderate exercise: This means getting "out there" and moving, every day. Starting up a thorough exercise program at least five days a week is a good place to begin, as is going for a walk after supper, or generally being more active. Spending the majority of your day sitting on a couch and doing nothing but watching television can leave your dream life lethargic and disconnected. When you get your body up and moving, you are moving your muscles and circulation system. This helps you stay as strong and healthy as possible so that you are ready for healthy sleep, by the end of the day.

• Set up a regular DreamStream ritual: having a regular ritual of doing this can make things a little bit easier so that you can remember more of your dreams.

• Write down some of your dreams. After you have some time to think about the dream and consider it a bit, try writing some of the details down. You can always come back to the dream and remember it again, helping to increase your connection to those dreams. Over time, you may start to remember your dreams with more details. This can make the future steps in the Dreamosophy approach easier. In addition, you may find that having details about these dreams can help you, because you can use them in the steps below, in case you can't remember a more recent dream.

As you begin this new approach to dreaming, remember that dreaming is natural and it is going to happen all on its own. When you approach your dreaming, you just let go. The dreams will do all the work if you let them, but if you are trying to force things and trying to make things twist around the way that you want, you may be sorely disappointed.

DREAMOSOPHY STEPS FOR REMEMBERING DREAMS

Now that you understand a little bit more about dreaming and what it all means, here are some simple steps to remembering more of your dreams. Remembering dreams can be a great experience. So much goes on during your dreams, and even if there doesn't seem to be a big message right away, through the Dreamosophy approach, you will learn to be free, feel good, to speak up, to make friends, and to learn something new every time. Remember, in the Dreamosophy approach, you are not going to force the situation. Let the dreams come to you and talk to you, but never try to force it along.

Dream Step 1

For the first step, keep in mind that you are interested in remembering your dreams. Don't just lie down at night and fall asleep. Actively tell yourself that you want to remember your dreams. You don't have to be forceful or fret over this, just keep it simple – tell yourself to remember your dreams – and then go to bed.

When you first wake up in the morning, do not move. Just lie there in bed, noticing how you feel. Is there a certain emotion that is lingering from the dream, such as confusion, happiness, sadness, anger, fear, joy, elation, or glee? Do you feel light, tired, heavy, or something else? Even if you aren't able to remember a dream at this point, you may still have some feelings that linger from the DreamStream, so taking notice of emotions and feelings may be important.

For the last two steps, consider talking with other people and being more social about your dreams. If you have a few people that you interact with daily, you can talk about your dreams with them. You may not remember the whole dream at first, but talking about the parts that you do remember is a great way to help you to remember more, later on. You can also ask at least at least one other person each day, if they remember their dreams, even if you aren't able to remember some of your own. This may seem silly, but when you interact with others about their dreams, and discuss some of your own, it becomes easier to remember your dreams later on.

This can become part of your bedtime routine. In addition to brushing your teeth, getting into your sleeping clothes, and reading a quick chapter before closing your eyes, consider coming up with a simple word or phrase to become deliberate and intentional about your dream aspirations. You could say something like, "I will remember my dreams. Remembering my dreams is important to me!" or "When I remember my dreams, I remember my self." Say this a few times each night before going to bed, and you may be surprised at how much this can help you to recall and appreciate dreams.

Some people feel that this step is not necessary and is just a lot of extra work for them. But if you are not deliberate in exploring your dreams, it is easy to forget your dedication; and your dreams may fade away before you can explore them. The rest of the steps in this guidebook may not be as successful if you don't step up and learn how to remember some of those dreams. Being deliberate, especially right before bed, can help you out. The good news is that it will only take a few minutes to repeat this mantra a few times, so you can easily get it done without too much trouble, and then go to bed.

Dream Step 2

Now we are going to consider your wake-up time. Are you someone who wakes up in the morning with the help of your alarm clock? If this is something that you do, you can make sure that you set the alarm clock to half an hour earlier each day. This allows you a chance to stay still in bed for a little longer and to observe some of the feelings that are around you. Or you can invest that time just reveling in the dream that you just had, not being forceful, but looking back through it like you would with a memory.

For those days that you don't have to get up with the help of an alarm clock, make sure that it doesn't wake you up. You can just allow the body to wake up without the help of an alarm, whenever it happens naturally for you. The later you are able to get up, the better. This allows you to get more dreaming in and can be amazing for helping you to realize what feelings are being elicited from the dreams.

The point here is to let the dream sink in for a while. When you are too focused on getting up and preparing for the activities of the day, it is easy to forget the dream completely. It may be evening by the time you think about your dream again and, by this time, you may have forgotten all about the dream. It is always best to think about your dream in the morning and, if you can, to allow yourself to wake up naturally so that you don't rush the process and can finish the dream.

Of course, there are times when you do have to get up and can't sleep in as long as you want. For these days, you may need the help of an alarm clock to wake you up early. Set your clock so that you get at least an extra thirty minutes to wake up and think about your dream. Think about the dream, replay it in your mind, and walk through it like a great memory that you want to enjoy. If you are able to go back through the dream a few times, this can be better because it helps to cement the dream in your mind.

You can do the same thing when you wake up naturally during the weekend or on days off, but you may be a bit more relaxed and won't have to worry about the time as much. Either way, make sure that you have enough time to replay the dream at least once and focus on the parts that seem important at the time so that you can remember the dream easier.

Dream Step 3

Before you go to sleep, make sure you have a pen or pencil and paper available. After you have some time to consider and reflect on some of the feelings that you have after dreaming, perhaps doing that for a few days or even weeks, just experiencing the feelings that wash around, over, and through you, then you can start writing them down. Try writing down the feelings and the sensations that you have when you first wake up after sleep.

This is not the time to remember all the details of your dreams. For this section, you are just exploring, or just being aware of how you feel and the sensations that are going on, when you dream and immediately after you wake up. You will explore remembering the dreams later on, but for now, you are just exploring the feelings and the sensations that are going on around you. Write down the thoughts, the feelings, and the sensations that you are having when you first wake up in the morning.

Over time, you may be able to start remembering your dreams because you are thinking about them so much. They may become more vivid and you can have a lot more fun with them. As you start to remember more parts about your dreams, it is fine if you start to write those down. Eventually, you may be able to consider the dreams and remember it all, even if you don't write them all down. But, some people need time to work up to this point.

After some time, you may want to find a friend or another dream buddy who is willing to share their dreams with you. You can both schedule a time that works and meet up with each other every week. You can then share the dreams that you had during the week with each other and explore the topics or ask questions to see what is going on. This can be an enjoyable experience for both of you. It allows you to talk about dreams and to share how far you have come. In the beginning, you may only be able to remember snippets of your dreams, but with some practice, and with the idea that you don't have to force the process at all, you may find that you remember more and more of your dreams.

Remembering your dreams just requires a little bit of attention. There's no need to force this to happen – you may be so busy in your days that you just jump into work and school and kids and don't even think about your dreams – but when you are able, actively remind yourself to remember your dreams before bed. Invest some time honoring the dreams by writing them down and letting the sensations surround you before getting up in the morning. Then, find a dream buddy and invest time talking about your dreams. These steps can make it much easier to feel that your dreams have value and can help you start remembering them. This can take time, but if you are gentle and start to allow the dreams to have more time and space in your life, you can start remembering more of your dreams, naturally.

IN SUMMARY

Remembering your dreams is an important step of the Dreamosophy approach. It is possible to do some of the exercises without remembering your dreams, but it is hard to get the deep connection and understanding that you need from your dreams if you can't remember them. It is best to focus on forming that connection with your dreams so you can remember them in detail before you move on to the other Dream Opportunities in this guidebook.

Luckily, it is pretty easy to start remembering your dreams, as long as you are deliberate in your actions. You must think about remembering your dreams before you go to bed. You must wake up a little bit earlier in the morning so you can concentrate on your dreams and keep them nearby, rather than running off to work the second you wake up and letting the dream get lost. You must also write down some notes about the dreams before getting up for the day. Writing down details that seem important, as well as some of the feelings you had with those dreams, makes things easier for you down the road.

In addition to writing things down to help you remember the dreams, there are a few other things that you can do. You can focus on the dreams for a few minutes each morning, rather than just getting out of bed right away. This one works similar to a memory; those memories that are the most prevalent in your mind are the ones that you think about the most. The same can be said about your dreams. If you think about them more, you may be able to remember them more.

You can also choose to use other options to help you get a good night of sleep and to ensure that you have some lucid dreams. Making sure that you have some water before bed, going to sleep at a good time each night, and getting into a routine to help you fall asleep and stay asleep all night may help make things easier. Being deliberate and reminding yourself to remember your dream each night before going to sleep may help you to have more vivid dreams that you may remember in the morning.

The more you focus on remembering your dreams and making it a part of your routine, the more dreams you may remember throughout your life. In the beginning, this seems simplistic and like something that will never work for you, but it does work; you can just keep exploring it and being open. Over time, your dreams may become more vivid and you may be able to remember them better than you could imagine.

This chapter invests some time talking about the different things that you can do to help remember your dreams. If you are someone who has trouble remembering your dreams, or you end up getting out of bed and ready for work too quickly so that the dream starts to fade, you may benefit from investing some extra time on this chapter. If you aren't able to hold onto the dreams you have, it is impossible to see results from this approach. It takes some hard work and dedication, but Dreamosophy has the potential to help you to learn from your dreams and feel satisfied about them each day. But first, remember them.

This exquisite pen-and-ink rendering of an anonymous 19th-Century woodcut was sent to the author by David Gonzales, a prisoner in California's San Quentin State Prison, in 1996. Since it came from inside a prison, it represents all the ways we are both imprisoned and able to obtain freedom in our dreams. The original rendering was drawn by hand, on an envelope, which was subsequently marred by a postmark. The digital version has been meticulously restored by Layout Designer Eduardo Lista Oleynick.

2: HOW TO BE FREE IN YOUR DREAMS

In the previous chapter, you invested some time reading about the myths that come with dreams and how you can explore remembering your dreams. While you also read about how the Dreamosophy approach doesn't include spending too much time interpreting and analyzing your dreams, this doesn't mean that there aren't some cool things that you can do in your dreams. In this chapter, you are going to be invited to consider some of the steps that you can take to learn how to be free in your dreams. There are a few levels in this chapter, but you may find that as you work through each one, you may be able to feel that freedom slowly come upon you in your dreams. So let's get started!

BE FREE IN YOUR DREAMS! LEVEL ONE

Being free in your dreams can take a little time and attention to complete. You first will be invited to notice the amount of freedom that you have in your dreams before moving on to identifying the freedom that you have in your dreams and your waking life. Once you complete these two levels, you can begin making the changes that you want so you have more freedom not only in your dreams, but also in your waking life.

In this first level, you don't need to try anything too crazy. The point is just to start to notice various aspects of your dream – just notice, that's all. In the past, when you dreamed you likely were just going along for the ride. You didn't worry about the actions that you took or the freedom you had to make decisions; and it's unlikely that you had very much influence over what happened in your dreams in the past. This is all about to change, but in this first level, just notice how you act in your dreams right now, before anything changes.

For this level, things are going to be kept pretty simple. You are not trying to force anything or learn some crazy things that will help you to be totally free in your dreams. In fact, all that you will be invited to do in this level is notice the dream opportunities. At this level, you are not working to make detailed connections between your waking life and your dreams. Instead, you are going to consider noticing if any of the opportunities that are in your dreams are the same opportunities that occur during your waking life.

Later, in Level 2, you will be invited to learn how to identify the basic Dream Opportunities.   You are basically learning a skill that you can use for the rest of your life. Then, in Level 3, you are going to learn how to transform these opportunities that you have noticed and identified, so that you are able to use them when you are waking.

As you explore these three levels, remember that while you are asleep, you are not trying to change your dreams. This can make sleeping and dreaming a lot of hard work, and none of us want that to happen. Instead, you may just want to notice things that are already present in your dreams, no matter what those things may be. To get started with this first level, there are a few exercises that you can do that may help you to understand how free you currently are in your life and in your dreams, so you can make an effort to change them if you are not happy with the outcome.

When we talk about being free, we are referring to the difference between being an active participant or a passive participant in your dream. Sometimes, when you go to sleep and when you dream, you may be a passive dreamer. You may not be aware of all the things you can do when you are dreaming; you just go along for the ride. In these passive dreams, you are watching what happens in front of you, but you haven't learned how to take the next step and decide what will happen. Through the Dreamosophy approach, you can learn to consider your dreams without any restrictions or constraints. Then you may be able to have total freedom.

We will get into more of that later, but for now, this level is just going to help you to learn how to notice your sense of freedom in your dream. It may help you to notice if you are restrained or free in the dream or if you are a passive or active participant. You will basically start looking at dreams that you remember, to see if you feel free or constrained. You will not consider what you can do about it, but rather, just notice what is happening at this point.

To start, you are going to take that dream journal or that pad and paper from earlier, and try to remember all your dreams for the next week. You can write them down, make up dreams, or record brief events from your waking life as if they were dreams. Just try to have a week's worth of dreams ready to go. Then, with each of the dreams, answer the following questions:

1. Are you as the dreamer active or passive in this dream?

2. Are you free or restrained in some way?

3. Do you have the starring role in this dream or a secondary part?

4. Do you like the way you are in this dream?

5. Are you participating in this dream or just observing?

6. What is the main form of activity in this dream?

7. List all the different roles (ways of doing things or talking or moving or acting) in this dream. Choose the one you like the most.

a.
b.
c.
d.

The whole point here is to learn how you react in your dreams. When you dream, what are the actions that you take? Are you just an observer, like watching a movie, without any control over what happens to you during that dream? For some people, this is a part of their life. They are used to being the observer without having any influence over what goes on around them. For others, this can be really frustrating because they want to have this control, but they just don't know how to get started. Just by noticing how you behave and the amount of freedom you currently have in your dreams, you may start to see some changes.

One thing that you may notice is that some aspects of your dreams can match with your waking life. For example, you may notice that the amount of freedom you have in your dreams is directly related to the amount of freedom you have in your waking life. So if your freedom is limited, you are not able influence what happens in the dream, and your feelings and actions have no influence on what occurs in the dream, then you are most likely experiencing the same amount of freedom in your waking life.

Later, you will learn how to make some changes to the amount of freedom you have in both your dream life and your waking life, but in this part, you are just investing the time to notice how much freedom is present in your dreams. So for a week or two, wake up in the morning and note how much freedom was present in your dreams. You can notice that each dream is a little bit different. In one dream, you may have more freedom, while in another dream, you have no freedom. This is perfectly fine, but write down the information and then average it out. This may help you with later exercises.

Over time, you may be able to change the way that you behave in the dreams. This can make it easier to remember your dreams. As you begin to remember more and more of your dreams, you may start to know yourself more as a dreamer. In fact, you may become more surprised at how much truth and intensity you have been holding in throughout your life. For this level, you are just starting to notice what goes on in your dreams, but over time, you may move on to being an active participant in your dreams and even to identifying how you can use your dreams to make changes in your life.

Waking Questions

Once you have some time to finish the dream and wake up, take a moment to go through a couple more questions. These may help you to start drawing some conclusions about your dreams and your real life.

1. Is your role in this dream similar to your role in waking?

2. Pause for a moment: Think about your level of freedom in work, play, and relationships.

You can pause for a moment and really think about this one. Think about how much freedom you have in your relationships, in work, in play, and in all the other things that you do during the day. Are you an active participant who gets to make decisions, or are you sitting on the sideline hoping that someone will tell you what to do? Often the dreams you have mirror your real life, and during this lesson, you be invited to consider that and understand how it works.

Teaching Someone Else

One thing that you may notice is that you may do better when you are able to teach someone else the things that you have just learned. You might consider finding a dream buddy, or at least a close friend or family member, who is willing to discuss dreams with you. Anybody you meet outside of your dreams can work well for this. Try using the three-foot or one-meter rule —anyone who is within three feet of you is the person you're supposed to talk with about dreams.

Get ready to invest some time talking to others about your dreams. They are likely to be just like you were when you first started this Dreamosophy process – they may want to know what everything means and why it is happening. But when you talk with them, you can bring up the five basic opportunities discussed in this guidebook:

- How to be free in your dreams
- How to feel good in your dreams
- How to speak up in your dreams
- How to make friends in your dreams
- How to understand and realize your dreams

Dream Opportunity Day:

One more exercise before we go on. For this one, you pick a time during the week to have a Dream Opportunity Day!

Make up an exercise that you think would help you have the dreams you want. Previously, you followed the Dreamosophy exercises. On this day, be inventive and make up your own. It can be anything. The kind of exercise is less important than doing it, because it is the doing that really helps you pay attention to your dreams.

During this time, you get to make up an exercise that may help you to have the dreams that you would like. Don't worry about getting the activity perfect; the actions are more important than the particular exercise, because it can help you to pay more attention to the dreams you are having. For example, you may decide that having a bowl of ice cream or saying a prayer before bed will help you to remember a dream. Or maybe jump up and down on one leg during the day, while eating a banana – you pick – just make sure that it is something that you are able and willing to do, and then compare the results the next day with how vivid and/or memorable your dreams are!

Basically, in Level 1, you are just considering your dreams and trying to get an idea of how free you are in your dreams. You are not making any changes at this time; you are simply relaxing and trying to notice if you are more active or more passive in your dreams. When you are able to notice how you react in your dreams, you can determine whether you like these results or not. Then, you can use some of the other levels in this section to help you gain more freedom, if you choose.

BE FREE IN YOUR DREAMS! LEVEL TWO

When you are done with Level 1 and have begun noticing what is going on in your dreams, you can move on to Level 2 – identifying and graphing aspects of your dreams. Level 1 was all about noticing things that were in your dream. In level 2, you are going to learn how to take things that happen in your daily life and things that happen in your dreams and identify how they can be connected. This is not a forced process, but rather it is one that can give you tools that can deepen and expand your experience and value of your own dream life.

Level 2 consists of a few exercises that can help you to identify important aspects of your dream life. These exercises are most beneficial if they are done when you remember a dream or when you have made one up that you want to use for Level 2. There are no right or wrong answers here, but just noticing some of the answers may help you to begin to see a difference in the dreams you are having. Through the Dreamosophy approach, you are going to start learning a new way of thinking about and experiencing your dreams. We are going to use these simple exercises as a way to start having dreams that work for you, rather than ones that work against you.

Exercise 1

First, invest a little time, to do a few exercises. These are going to help you see how free you are in your dreams. You can choose to do this after each dream and just invest a few minutes on it, or you can take longer to write each dream and write out longer answers and responses to each of the exercises and questions. To start, take into consideration some of the dreams you have had recently.

To begin identifying, start by GRAPHING your freedom. Use this scale to rate your level of freedom. How active are you in this dream?

1. NOT ACTIVE: You take no action in the dream.
2. PASSIVE: You are only a part of the dream. Your ability to control is that of someone who is present but uninvolved and unresponsive.
3. SLIGHTLY ACTIVE: There is some response by you to dream events, but for the most part your activity does not change the outcome of the dream.
4. ACTIVE: Your activity is obvious in the dream. Your actions in response to events are effective.
5. VERY ACTIVE: Your activity is central to the dream.

Next to your notes about this dream, write the number that corresponds to your level of activity in your dream life generally. GENERAL ACTIVITY: 1, 2, 3, 4, or 5.

Also next to your notes about this dream, write the number that corresponds to your level of activity in this dream. RECENT DREAM ACTIVITY: 1, 2, 3, 4, or 5.

When you were a younger child, how much freedom did you really have to do the things that you wanted? Sure, you didn't have any bills to pay or have to go to work, but your decisions were minimal and your parents usually did the decision making. On the other hand, as you grow into adulthood, you gain more freedom and the path that your life takes is going to be connected to the decisions that you make. This freedom sometimes decreases again when you reach your older years as you need more assistance from other people to get things done.

Your dreams can go through ebbs and flows as well. In some dreams, you may be in the passenger seat and others you may be totally free to participate however you choose, even before you go through these levels. But over time, you can choose your level of freedom in the dream, without feeling that it is forced, because this helps you to get the most out of your dreams.

Exercise 2

Past Questions:

1. Using the 1-to-5 scale given earlier, on a new page or sheet of paper, write the number for your waking activity that best indicates the amount of freedom you had during the following periods of your life:

1 - 5 years old
6 - 12 years old
13 - 16 years old
17 - 21 years old
22 - 25 years old
26 - 35 years old
36 - 45 years old
46 - 55 years old
56 - 65 years old
66 - 75 years old
76 years and older

2. Now draw vertical and horizontal lines and numbers to create this graph of your freedom for each period of your life. Place a dot above each age, then connect the dots:

5

4

3

2

1

age   1   6   13 17 22 26 36 46 56 66 76

Your chart will look something like this:

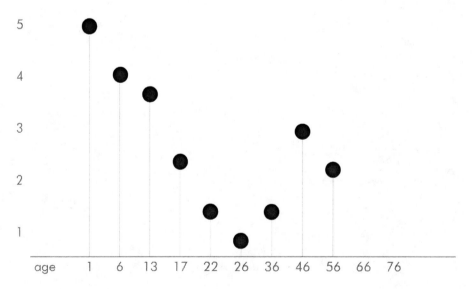

Your completed graph might look something like this after you connect the dots:

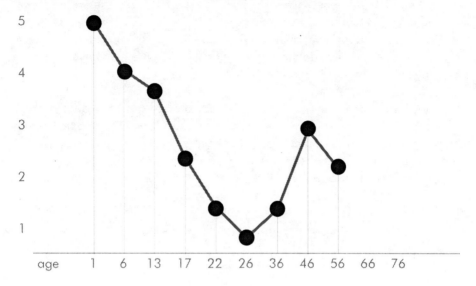

- Now look at the last graph.
- Notice if your freedom has changed over the years.
- Think about what has happened to you, how you have changed.

3. Think about how your parents, your friends, and your neighborhood have determined your ability to be free in your life.

4. Are you satisfied with the freedom you have in waking?

5. Write down three beliefs you have about how you should be in waking:

a._____
b._____
c._____

Dream Opportunity Question

What special strengths do you have that you don't use?

For this exercise, invest some time to understand the special strengths that you have and to look a bit more deeply into yourself. To start, think about some of the special strengths that you have that you don't often use. Everyone has strengths that are important to character, but perhaps you are worried that others are going to judge you or that you aren't really good at those strengths, so you just end up pushing them down deep into dim memories, hopes, and dreams. But, why do you do that? Are you really being the best person you can be, when you hide some of your personal strengths?

You may not realize it, but with this exercise, you are being asked a question that may seem a little bit out of your comfort zone – a question most people tend to avoid. People may often blame themselves for being a certain way, without ever realizing that they were forced to be that way as they grew up. Now, as a grown up, you may be able to make that change. You can start by understanding the Dreamosophy Dream Opportunities. You may be able to find hidden talents through your dreams, and you may be able to gain the skills and the know-how you need to realize your fondest dreams in waking life.

Bonus Exercises

Past: In any of your dreams, identify and list the ways in the dreams that you felt, acted, and thought that were the way you were as a child.

Present: Try to identify in your most recent dream a single way of talking, feeling, acting, or understanding that is completely yours the way you are now.

Future: Consider how you could have changed or completed your most recent dream:
• How could you have changed the actions you used in the dream?
• How could you have changed your level of feeling?
• How could you have changed how much you spoke up?
• How could you have changed your level of understanding?
• How could you have changed the level of contact you had with other people in the dream?

Sometimes, taking another look at the dream you are in and seeing it from a different point of view can make it completely different. For example, if you had a dream where you were a child who thought differently than you do now, it may be helpful to use some of your knowledge and understanding from today to apply to your dream. This may help you see some things that you missed out on before. If you felt lost and confused in the dream, you can bring in some of the future and think about how you would have changed what happened in the dream.

BE FREE IN YOUR DREAMS! LEVEL THREE

Unlike other how-to books about dreams, this one is not going to promise that you can get miraculous results with no activity. This how-to asks you to make some big changes in the way that you understand and consider your dreams, and the difference can be tremendous.

In this last level, there are a few exercises for you to explore. They invite you to consider a change. You will move on from the noticing that you did in the first level and the identifying in the second level. This third level will focus on changing and producing transformation.

So far this guidebook has given you some introductory exercises and theories to follow. Hopefully, you have been doing these exercises, but you have probably noticed that you have not received any real explanation for what all the exercises mean and what results you should get out of these exercises.

The good news is that if you just dedicate yourself to the exercises that are provided on each level, you can notice that your dreams are developing simply and naturally. You don't have to force this to happen. You don't have to spend a lot of energy or hassle to invite your dreams to change and develop. You can just focus on some of the exercises and use them to help your dreams develop on their own.

The reason that this guidebook has not spent too much time focusing on the explanation of the exercises and the developments that you may experience is that the experiences themselves are going to be more important than the explanations. Each person will go through this process in a different way. So, just doing the exercises on your own, letting your dreams develop how they may, can make a big difference.

In Level 3, we are going to take another shift. These three levels have changed so much. You started out with just noticing the things in your dream, which, for those who are just getting started, can be a challenge in itself. Then the second level moved on to identifying and rating some of the things in your dream and how they could pertain to your daily life. Now, you are done being an observer and you can engage more actively in Level 3. This level helps you change your dreams simply by changing your opportunities.

In Level 3, you will be invited to defy some of your own personal limits. These limits are going to be different for everyone, so while some may have an easy time doing this, you may find it is more of a challenge. Be gentle with yourself and remain calm, because departing from your usual expectations of yourself can be difficult for some people; but with some deliberation, you may be able to achieve it in no time.

Part three may be more difficult than the other two parts. This is because you will begin introducing some of your Dream Opportunities into your daytime life. It is not just about dreaming now; instead, it is about bringing those opportunities to life and seeing how they can make a difference. If you aren't trying anything new when you are awake, your progress is probably going to stop. But, keep in mind that if you try too much at once, you could start feeling discouraged. So, take things at a pace that is right for you and be gentle with yourself during this process.

A quick warning before you start: Moving on to Level 3 and doing some of the activities that are suggested in this level may produce some changes in your life. You are solely responsible for these changes. If you are dedicated and work at a pace that is comfortable for you, it may be easier for you to see some of the changes that you want. On the other hand, if you skip steps or don't give them the time that you might, you may not see the changes you hope for.

To maintain the proper balance in this step, be careful to maintain some proper limits to your total freedom in your waking life. If you are having trouble finding some of this balance in your waking life, or if you are not sure about what is proper, ask a certified and licensed professional for help. By progressing to Level 3, you are agreeing to accept full and total responsibility for your life. If you don't feel that you can handle this responsibility, do not continue to Level 3 at this time. Once again, let yourself try new steps gradually. If you are not comfortable, stop or ask for help.

Now that you know a few of the instructions for this level, you can learn how to use Level 3 to add some freedom to your dream life. For this part, either make up or remember your dream. You can repeat the steps in the previous chapter, or write down the dreams, to help you remember them for this step.

Take that dream and then consider your freedom. Here are a few of the questions to ask yourself:

1. Are you satisfied with your level of freedom in this dream?

2. What would have to happen in this dream so that you could be totally satisfied with your freedom in the dream?

3. What is your main activity in this dream?

4. How do you keep your freedom incomplete?

5. What would you have to do to have complete freedom?

6. Does your freedom in this dream work for you or against you?

7. How would you have to change your level of freedom to flow through to a whole new level?

8. Rate your freedom level in this dream using the 1 to 5 scale given in Level 2.

How active are you in this dream?

1. NOT ACTIVE: You take no action in the dream.
2. PASSIVE: You are only a part of the dream. Your ability to control is that of someone who is present but uninvolved and unresponsive.
3. SLIGHTLY ACTIVE: There is some response by you to dream events, but for the most part your activity does not change the outcome of the dream.
4. ACTIVE: Your activity is obvious in the dream. Your actions in response to events are effective.
5. VERY ACTIVE: Your activity is central to the dream.

What would it be like if you took your level of freedom one level higher?
What would it be like if you took your level of freedom one level lower?

9. List all your fears of what would happen if you raised your freedom to a total level.

Finding Your Dream Freedom Word

Write the ten main words you could use to describe what is happening in your dream.

1. _____
2. _____
3. _____
4. _____
5. _____
6. _____
7. _____
8. _____
9. _____
10. _____

Circle five of the words on your list of ten.

From the five circled words, write three on a new page.

1. _____
2. _____
3. _____

Of the three words, circle two.

From the two circled words, write one on a blank page, all by itself. That single word is your Dream Freedom Word. Remember your Dream Freedom Word throughout the day.

There doesn't have to be much rhyme or reason to the word that you picked; just go with the word that makes sense for you or the one that stands out the most through these different stages. This single word is your Dream Freedom Word. Keep track of this word. Think about it a few times throughout the day, whether you pull out that piece of paper on which you wrote down the word or just think about it.

Waking Suggestion

Here is your waking suggestion for this level: For this one, pick a day where you can change your level of activity. As you begin to notice how active you are, consider increasing or decreasing your level of activity at regular intervals, and continue to do so for the rest of the day. This can help you gain more freedom during the day and may translate into more freedom when you go to sleep and dream at night. Be responsible and respectful in all your actions when you are awake and do not harm yourself or others in any way.

1. Try to change your level of activity today. As you notice how active you are, lessen it a little and then increase it. Try this out all day long, lessen it a little and then increase it. Be respectful and responsible in all your actions in waking life. Do not harm yourself or others in any way.

2. Before you go on, did you really try out some of those new things? If not, at least notice and identify how you stopped yourself.

Did you get confused?
Less active?
Did you restrict your ability to feel good?
Did you speak up less?

Maintaining the Changes

If you have done the exercises in Levels 1, 2, and 3, your dreams have probably begun to change already. Here is a series of questions you can use to maintain the changes:

1. How did you like the freedom you had in this dream?

2. What is the dream trying to tell you about your waking life?

3. What is this dream trying to tell you about your future?

4. How can you change your opportunity so that the present and future circumstances work for you?

If you are not satisfied with your freedom in your dreams, repeat the exercises in Level 3 on a different day, with a different dream. If you are still not satisfied, repeat them again, on yet another day.

When you are done with the three levels in this chapter, you may notice a huge change in the amount of freedom that you can enjoy in your dreams. You may not just be an innocent bystander who just gets to watch what is happening and doesn't get a say. Now you may notice that there is a distinct difference in your dreams and the amount of freedom that you have to move around, make decisions, and do the things that you want in your dreams.

IN SUMMARY

Many times, the amount of freedom that you have in your dreams will be directly related to the amount of freedom that you have in your waking life. You may go through life feeling like you have to wait on the decisions of others, or that someone else is always taking center stage and you are just going along for the ride. But, there are things that you can do to change this and to make sure that you are the focus, if that is what you want.

First, start noticing that you don't have the freedom that you want. This chapter began with noticing how much freedom you have in your dreams. This is often a good indicator of how much freedom you have in your waking life as well. At this level, all you were invited to do was notice how much freedom was present in your dreams. It varies at times, and there may be dreams where you have more freedom, but you should be able to average them out to get an estimate of your freedom levels in your dreams. In this first step, you are simply responsible for noticing your levels of freedom.

As you progressed through the three levels in this chapter, you were invited to take some actions. Not only did you notice your level of freedom in your dreams, but you were also invited to begin to notice how much freedom you have in your daily life. You may be surprised to realize that your level of freedom is not as high as you would like. That is fine for the first two levels, but by the third level, you are responsible for using these connections and making some changes. Over time, you can change the level of freedom that you have in your dreams by changing your awareness of your freedom level in your waking life.

Having more freedom in your dreams can change so much. Instead of being a bystander, or someone who sits back and watches what is going on with the dream, without any influence over it at all, you may learn how to become the star attraction in your dream, if that is what you prefer. You may be able to move the story along, speak up the way that you want, and move around in the dream in any fashion that you want. You won't be stuck doing whatever another person or thing in the dream tells you to do any longer, because you will be the one choosing your level of freedom both inside and outside of your dream.

The amount of freedom that you have in your waking life and your dream life can strongly affect the quality of life that you get to enjoy. With the help of the steps in this chapter, you can gain more freedom in both and see the results shine out in very little time!

When you are ready to gain more freedom in your dreams, such as the freedom to move around and do as you would like in the dream, make sure to go through the three levels in this chapter. You may see some huge changes very quickly!

3: HOW TO FEEL GOOD IN YOUR DREAMS

In this part of the guidebook, you will be invited to focus on how you feel in your dreams. It is likely that in the past, you woke up from your dreams with some kinds of lingering feelings. You may have awakened feeling sad or angry or even happy after the dream based on what occurred during your dream. Or, you may have awakened feeling that something was off in the dream or that there may be a lesson you could learn from it. There are so many different feelings that can come from your dreams, but as you will see with this guidebook, you can influence some of the feelings that occur while dreaming.

Let's consider the feelings that are associated with your dreams. The levels below start with noticing some of the feelings that you have in real life and in your dreams. Then, you will move on to identifying some of the feelings that come in your dreams, before moving on to the final level that helps you to transform your feelings in your dreams and in your life. Let's consider the three levels of feeling good in your dreams and how you can control your feelings in every dream!

FEEL GOOD IN YOUR DREAMS! LEVEL 1

In this first level, we are going to consider how you can feel in your dreams. There are often some strong feelings in your dreams. There are times where you may have awakened from your dreams feeling sad, upset, or even happy with what went on during the dream. Through these exercises, you can start influencing how you feel and how intensely you feel in your dreams, rather than just going along for the ride. You will learn more about this later on, in Level 3. For Level 1, you are just going to learn how to recognize some of these feelings, to let them wash over you from the moment that you wake up, rather than ignoring them or trying to push them away as you get going on your day.

With the Dreamosophy approach, when you hear about feelings, it is about how you feel as the dreamer (such as how you feel after the dream is done and feelings you notice), about how other characters in the dream feel, and how the dream may feel to you overall. This level invites you to consider how you feel in your dreams, and for now, you will just notice those feelings, whether these feelings are indifferent, bad, or good.

Before you get started on this section, remember or make up your dream. You can follow some of the tips in the first chapter, How to Remember Your Dreams, to help you remember your dream. You may want to use a different dream every day, or you may find it helpful to go back to the same dream throughout a whole week or longer.

Once you have a dream that you want to use, you can answer the following questions:

1. How strongly do you feel in this dream?
2. What is the overall feeling in this dream?
3. What feelings do you as the dreamer have in this dream?
4. List all the different feelings in this dream, putting the strongest first:
   a._____
   b._____
   c._____
   d._____

Waking Questions

Now that you have those questions answered for the dreams that you had over the past week, you can ask a few questions when you are awake, including the following:

1. Think about all the feelings you had today:

a. Which was the strongest?
b. The weakest?

2. List some of the different feelings you normally do NOT have:

a._____
b._____
c._____
d._____

3. What feelings do you have about yourself?

a. Do you like yourself?
b. Do you like some things and dislike others?

4. Are there some ways you would like to feel in the dream but you just can't or don't feel that way for different reasons?

5. In waking?

6. Make a mental or written note of them.

The more you realize what your feelings are, both in your dreams and in real life, the more you may be able to guide them in ways that work for you. For now, you are simply noticing the feelings that come up and recording them for later consideration.

Dream Opportunity Day

Sometime while you're considering this Dream Opportunity, take a Dream Opportunity Day. Make up an exercise that you think would help you have the dreams you want. Previously, you followed the Dreamosophy exercises. On this day, be inventive and make up your own. It can by anything. The kind of exercise is less important than doing it, because it is the doing that really helps you pay attention to your dreams.

FEEL GOOD IN YOUR DREAMS! LEVEL 2

After you invest about a week on Level 1, remembering your dreams and noticing the different feelings that you have in your dreams, and once you feel comfortable with these processes, you can benefit from moving on to Level 2. Just as you did when exploring freedom in your dreams, you are going to move from noticing in Level 1 to being more active and identifying in Level 2.

Exercise 1

During this level, you are invited to extend your knowledge of your dreams by rating what is going on and then graphing your levels of feelings. You can start by identifying your dreams and how intensely you feel about them. You can then graph the feelings you have based on each dream. Every day for a week or two, remember your dreams and then give each dream a number between 1 and 5, based on the following scale.

Generally, taking all of your dreams into consideration, how intensely do you feel in your dreams?

1. NO FEELING: Your dreams are about things or events that remain neutral.
2. SLIGHT: Your dreams contain some feeling, but the feeling is vague and in the background.
3. MODERATE: Your dreams contain some feeling that is not vague; but the feeling does not dominate or even greatly influence your dream.
4. STRONG: Your dreams contain definite feeling, more than is usually evident in your waking life; but the feeling is not central to the dream.
5. INTENSE: The feeling overrides all else in the dream. You are aware that you are feeling and allow it to occur fully.

Next to your notes about this dream, write the number that corresponds to your level of feeling in your dream life generally. GENERAL FEELING: 1, 2, 3, 4, or 5.

Also next to your notes about this dream, write the number that corresponds to your level of feeling in this dream. RECENT DREAM FEELING: 1, 2, 3, 4, or 5.

As you move through Level 2, you can invest some time looking at the different levels of feelings that you have when you are going about your normal day. Are you happy with the level of feelings that you are having in your life? What about the levels of feelings that you've had in the different phases of your life up to now? Are you able to see that they go up and down based on your age and the events that happened at each life phase? You may notice that your levels of feelings go up and down in life, as they do in your dreams. At this level, you have the opportunity to explore increasing the level of feelings, especially good feelings, in your dreams, so that you can enjoy your dreams much more.

Exercise 2

Past Questions:

1. Using the 1-to-5 scale given earlier, on a new sheet, page, or screen, write the number for your waking activity that best indicates the intensity of feeling you had during the following periods of your life:

1 - 5 years old
6 - 12 years old
13 - 16 years old
17 - 21 years old
22 - 25 years old
26 - 35 years old
36 - 45 years old
46 - 55 years old
56 - 65 years old
66 - 75 years old
76 years and older

2. Now draw vertical and horizontal lines and numbers to create this graph of your feeling for each period of your life. Place a dot above each age, then connect the dots.

5

4

3

2

1

age   1   6   13   17   22   26   36   46   56   66   76

Your chart will look something like this:

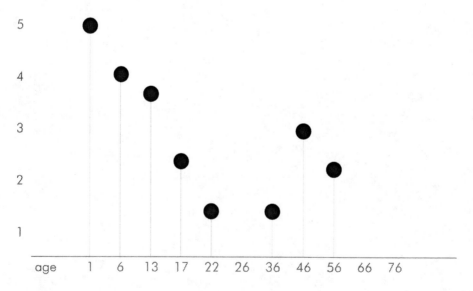

Your completed graph might look something like this after you connect the dots:

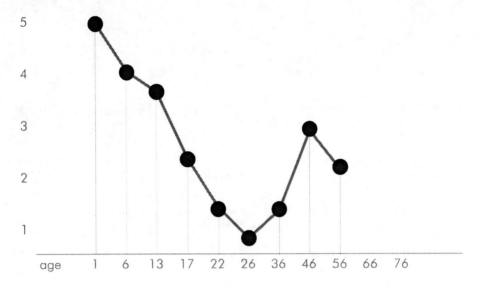

* Now look at the graph.
* Notice if your feeling has changed over the years.
* Think about what has happened to you, how you have changed.

3. Think about how your parents, your friends, and your neighborhood may have determined your ability to experience feeling in your life.

4. Are you satisfied with the level of intensity of feeling you have in waking?

5. List what kinds of feelings were allowed as you were growing up, and what kinds were frowned upon.

ALLOWED:

a._____

b._____

c._____

FROWNED UPON:

a. _____

b. _____

c. _____

Dream Opportunity Question

Are there times when you stop yourself from feeling good? What would it be like if you felt as good as you would like to?

Whether or not you know it, you have been asked to think about things that most people try to avoid. Often people blame themselves for being a certain way without ever realizing that they were forced to be that way as they grew up and that now, if they could understand their Dream Opportunities, they could change.

This can be difficult for some people to handle. You may feel bad that you aren't happy in your current life or that you aren't in control of your feelings right now. You may have been taught in life to go to work and pay the bills. These activities don't necessarily make you have strong feelings. But, with some practice, you may be able to change this, and learn how to have better feelings in your waking life and in your dreams.

Bonus Exercises

These bonus exercises can help you identify some of your feelings in your dreams, as well as in your waking life.

Past: In any of your dreams, identify and list the ways in the dreams that you felt, acted, and thought that were the way you were as a child.

Present: Try to identify in your most recent dream a single way of talking, feeling, acting, or understanding that is completely yours the way you are now.

Future: Consider how you could have changed or completed your most recent dream:

- How could you have changed the actions you used in the dream?
- How could you have changed your level of feeling?
- How could you have changed how much you spoke up?
- How could you have changed your level of understanding?
- How could you have changed the level of contact you had with other people in the dream?

These three exercises are meant to get you focused on the different feelings that are going on in your dreams, as well as the feelings that you have in your waking life. When you look at your feelings, you can become more aware of them, and over time, you may even be able to control these emotions. How great will it feel to have good dreams, dreams that make you feel happy, rather than feeling indifferent, angry, or even scared during your dreams?

Remember, in this level you are only identifying the different emotions and feelings that show up in your dreams. You are not looking to make any changes at this point. It is all about identifying and recognizing these emotions and understanding how they relate to your waking life.

FEEL GOOD IN YOUR DREAMS! LEVEL 3

In this final level, you will shift from identifying your feelings to transforming them. During the first two levels, the exercises were set up to help you learn and explore in preparation for Level 3. During this level, you will learn how to transform your dreams by transforming your opportunities.

Now that you have invested some time recognizing the feelings that you have in your dreams, you can explore changing the way that you feel in your waking life and your dream life. At this point, you have invested some time exploring the different feelings that have in your dreams, through the exercises and opportunities of the first two levels. Now, you are going to be invited to explore how to feel good in your dreams. The questions that you can ask yourself after your dreams this week include:

1. Are you satisfied with the way you feel in this dream?
2. What would have to happen in the dream so that you could be totally satisfied with the way you feel in the dream?
3. What is your main feeling in this dream?
4. How do you keep yourself from feeling as good as you would like?
5. What would you have to do or what would you have to change, for you to feel completely good?
6. Does the way you feel in this dream work for you or against you?
7. How would you have to change the way you feel to flow through to a whole new level?
8. Rate the INTENSITY with which you feel your feelings, using the 1 – 5 scale given in Level 2.

Generally, taking all of your dreams into consideration, how intensely do you feel in your dreams?

> 1. NOT FEELING: Your dreams are about things or events that remain neutral.
> 2. SLIGHT: Your dreams contain some feeling, but the feeling is vague and in the background.
> 3. MODERATE: Your dreams contain some feeling that is not vague; but the feeling does not dominate or even greatly influence your dream.
> 4. STRONG: Your dreams contain definite feeling, more than is usually evident in your waking life; but the feeling is not central to the dream.
> 5. INTENSE: The feeling overrides all else in the dream. You are aware that you are feeling and allow it to occur fully.

> What would it be like if you took your level of feeling one level higher?
> What would it be like if you took your level of feeling one level lower?

9. What good things might happen if you began to have more feeling in your life?

Finding Your Dream Feeling Word

Write the ten main words you could use to describe what is happening in your dream.

1. _____
2. _____
3. _____
4. _____
5. _____
6. _____
7. _____
8. _____
9. _____
10. _____

Circle five of the words on your list of ten.

From the five circled words, write three on a new page.

1. _____
2. _____
3. _____

Of the three words, circle two.

From the two circled words, write one on a blank page, all by itself. That single word is your Dream Feeling Word. Remember your Dream Feeling Word throughout the day.

Waking Suggestion

1. Try to change your level of feeling today. As you notice how strongly you feel, lessen it a little and then increase it. Try this out all day long, lessen it a little and then increase it. NOTE: Don't try to change WHAT you feel, just how INTENSELY you feel. Be respectful and responsible in all your actions in waking life. Do not harm yourself or others in any way.
2. Before you go on, did you really try out some of those new things? If not, at least notice and identify how you stopped yourself:
Did you get confused?
Less active?

Did you restrict your ability to feel good?
Did you speak up less?
Did you pull away from contact?

Remember that during this phase, you do not want to change what you are feeling, just the intensity of the feelings. Of course, be responsible and respectful with all your actions during your waking life. If changing your feelings at a particular moment is going to harm you or another person, do not attempt it at all. When you practice influencing your feelings in waking life, that influence may show up in your dream life as well.

You may find that each day your emotions are a little different. Some days you may feel tired, while others you may feel energetic. There may be days when you are going to be sad or angry, and other days when you may feel happy. This is not the time to change the feelings that you have. Right now, you are just taking some time to explore the intensity of your feelings, no matter what they are. If you feel happy, take the emotion and consider what it might be like to move it up and down in intensity.

This exercise gives you the opportunity to change and be in control of your emotions. You may be used to just experiencing your emotions, without getting a chance to really decide how you will feel. During this time, you may notice that some of your emotions don't make much sense or that you are overreacting to some of the situations that occur during your life. In the beginning, just focus on taking those emotions and moving them up and down in intensity.

Over time, you can make some different changes to how your emotions affect you and even how you react to different situations, but first, it can be helpful to gain some control over the intensity that your emotions have. You may find that this transition happens naturally for you, or that you can do it without even noticing. Keep it easy and just focus on changing the intensity of your emotions before exploring anything else.

With some practice, you may be able to take the control you've cultivated in your waking life and move it over to your dreams. Think of how nice it would feel to be able to be happy in your waking life as well as in your dream life!

Maintaining the Changes

If you have done the exercises in Levels 1, 2, and 3, your dreams have probably begun to change already. Here is a series of questions you can use to maintain the changes:

1. How did you like the feelings you had in this dream?
2. What is the dream trying to tell you about your waking life?
3. What is this dream trying to tell you about your future?
4. How did you like the way you felt in this dream?
5. How can you change your opportunity so that the present and future circumstances in the story work for you?

If you are not satisfied with how you feel in your dreams, repeat the exercises in Level 3 on a different day, with a different dream. If you are still not satisfied, repeat them again, on yet another day. You can also return to the exercises in Levels 1 and 2, for greater insight and sensitivity. Keep repeating, until your dreams provide additional insight and guidance.

Doing this occasionally can help maintain the work that you've put in during these three levels. If, at any time, you are not satisfied with the results you get, try again on a different day with a new dream. Everyone has a different pace, and it is possible that you may benefit from going through these levels a few times, to get comfortable with them. Try not to feel frustrated. As you explore these simple steps, you can continue to get the benefits of influencing your feelings in your dreams!

IN SUMMARY

Learning how to feel good in your dreams can help you enjoy your dreaming more than ever. Many times when you dream, you are just a passenger along for the ride. The feelings you have in your dreams may all too often be anger, sadness, or other unpleasant feelings that aren't much fun. Learning how to feel good in your dreams can take some time and attention, but it can also be very rewarding for both your dream life and your waking life.

In the first section, you were invited to focus on just noticing the feelings that you had in your dreams. If you've just been an innocent bystander so far in your dreams, this section offered the opportunity to be a little more active and notice what feelings you experience in your dreams. It doesn't matter what these feelings are at this point, simply notice which ones you are dealing with. Often the feeling you notice first is indifference, which is fine. There are no right or wrong feelings to have in your dreams. Just take notice of the feelings you experience.

Once you have begun to notice what kinds of feelings you experience in your dreams, you can start making some identifications. You can consider your daily waking life and see what kinds of feelings you have as you move through the day. Often these feelings are going to be pretty similar to what you experience in your dreams. Perhaps you didn't notice that you had these feelings, but that's one of the great things about this Dreamosophy approach – you get to notice your life in a whole new way.

In the third level, you were invited to make some changes in your waking life. You were invited to influence your feelings, deciding which way you prefer for them to be, whether you are happy or sad, as well as how intense some of these feelings are. These simple changes can help you to feel better in your waking life, and this can translate back into your dream life as well. It may take some time to practice influencing those feelings – especially if you have been holding onto them for a long time – but with patience and practice, you have the opportunity to enjoy your life – and your dreams – more than ever before.

These three levels may take some time to master, and that's fine. Once you feel comfortable with what you've done, you may benefit from the steps given to help you maintain what you've accomplished. It can be easy to fall back into some of the distracting habits and less-than-desirable feelings that you had before. If you want to maintain those new feelings in your waking life and in your dream life, maintain your focus. Going back and reviewing some of the levels and using the tips provided can help make this easier for you.

When you are able to feel good in your dreams, it may also mean you have been able to change the way that you feel in your waking life. Remember that your dream life includes snippets of what happens in your waking life, that often show up in your dream life as well, so when you change one, you change the other. When you are able to influence the feelings that you have in your waking life, and you are able to influence your feelings in ways that are satisfying for you, you are able to enjoy life more; and in turn, you may enjoy your dreams more as well.

It is possible to influence your feelings, even in your dreams, through learning to influence these feelings when you are awake as well. By following the three levels presented in this chapter, you can let go of the feelings of sadness or indifference or other less-than-desirable feelings and replace them with some of the preferred feelings you have been seeking!

4: HOW TO SPEAK UP IN YOUR DREAMS

Chapter 4 presents the Dream Opportunity: How to Speak Up in Your Dreams. You may often find that you are just a bystander in your dreams. In many instances, you do not make much of an impact at all because you are just there to watch. Sometimes, as the dreamer, you will be watching the dream as if you were watching it on a movie screen. You won't participate in the dream at all, and any actions that you take in the dream may have absolutely no effect on how the dream turns out.

Another way that you may experience the dream is as someone who is in the dream – you may participate, but with very little activity. Although you are taking action, your actions don't influence the dream in any substantial way. Often, there is someone else creating the action in the dream. In fact, it is unlikely that you even speak during these dreams. Any words that you do say during the dream have no consequences and are basically meaningless.

If this is the way that you dream, you may think this is normal. You may not understand the powerful impact that you can have in your dreams, much less that there is an opportunity for you to speak up and change what happens in the dream. Some of those who understand the power they have over their dreams may still find it hard to speak up during dreams.

For some reason, speaking up in dreams can be hard for many people to master. Perhaps this is because they have such a hard time speaking up in their daily lives. Remember that there are many connections between your waking life and your dream life, so when you have issues in your dreams about speaking up and influencing, it may be because you are struggling with the same issues in your waking life. When you make some changes in your waking life, it becomes easier for you to speak up in your dreams and in your waking life.

When you hear about speaking up in this guidebook, it basically means making some noise in your dreams, literally or figuratively. It's not enough to just sit back and let things happen in your dreams without any noise. In this Opportunity – How to Speak Up, you will be invited to learn how to make some noise and how to express yourself in your dreams, because this can be so powerful!

SPEAK UP IN YOUR DREAMS! LEVEL ONE

In this first level, you will be invited to start noticing some of the sounds that are in your dreams. When you become passive in your dreams and just let them happen, you are missing out on so much. Instead, try noticing the different noises that go on around you. Often, these noises get pushed to the back of the mind because they don't seem that important. When you think about the dream the next morning, it is unlikely that you will think about the noises that went on or what you said during the dream; it is more likely that you will find yourself focusing on the images and the people in your dreams.

To begin, consider one of your recent dreams. Consider it without the pictures, images, or people that may have been involved. Instead, think about the expressions that were in your dreams. When you are able to take away some of the images, you may notice that your dreams have a lot of loud sounds in them. One major sound that you may miss out on is your own voice. You may not make any noise in your dream. You may sit back and just watch the dream, without using your own voice, without expressing yourself, or perhaps barely speaking at all.

When this guidebook discusses noise, it refers both to how you make noise as the dreamer, and also the other noises that occur during the dream. These other noises can mean just as much as the noise that you are making, so it can be helpful to pay attention to them. What are some of the different noises that you hear? What are other people saying to you? What background noise is there in the activities of the dream? Think about what others are telling you in the dream, and what other noises are around you. This is your opportunity to begin identifying your dreams by sounds, noises, or other forms of expression, rather than just by the images that you see.

At this level, it's enough just to notice the noise that is in your dream. This can be hard to do. There is a lot of noise that goes on in all your dreams, but since you aren't focusing on these noises, you may be missing out on them. Guiding yourself to listen to the sounds of your dream and recognizing what they are may make a big difference in your dreams, and may even help you to speak up more in your waking life. You will learn more about this later.

For now, just notice the different noises that are in your dreams. There may be loud and soft noises, beautiful and dissonant, they may come from many sources. There may be a great deal of communication and expression that goes on between the different actors in your dreams. When you notice these noises, you may also want to look at other ways that you communicate in the dream, such as through gardening, art, dancing, signs, and proffering food. By noticing both the noises that you make and other ways that you communicate, your opportunities to speak up may increase.

So, to get started, it's important to remember at least one of your dreams. Try doing this for about a week with a new remembered dream each day, making up a dream on any of the days that you can't recall one. Remember, having a good memory of the dream can be easier if you write it down. Once you are ready, answer the following questions for your dream:

1. How much do you speak, make noise, or express yourself in this dream?

2. What is your main way of making noise or expressing yourself?

3. Is your speaking and communication the main expression in the dream? Or is something or someone else more important?

4. List all the different ways of making noise or expressing yourself in this dream, the most important first:

a) _____

b) _____

c) _____

d) _____

These questions may provide you with great insight on how you express yourself in your dreams. In the beginning, your voice and your expressions may be limited. It is likely that someone else takes the reins and is in charge of how the conversation goes or what actions happen in the dream. The aspiration at this level is simply to notice what is happening in regard to how and if you speak up in your dreams.

In the beginning, you may notice that your expressions in the dreams are limited. You might not have much to say at this time; and you may just sit back and watch the dream unfold, rather than being an active participant. Simply bringing to your attention things in your dreams, such as the level of activity and expression, may help to refocus your mind. You may notice that you aren't that happy with the expression you are giving in your dreams, and this alone may help to spur the dreams to work the way that you would like.

Waking Questions

Now that you have had some time to notice your expressions in your dreams, you can bring some of this noticing out into the open. It is likely that there are connections between how you experience self-expression in your dreams and how you experience self-expression in your waking life. Forming this connection, which you can start to do just by noticing at this time, may help you to make some changes in both your waking life and your dream life.

You are encouraged to ask and focus on the following questions when you are awake, to help you form some of the connections that you need at this point:

1. Is this the same style of speaking and expression you use in waking?

2. Do you like the way you are speaking or expressing yourself in this dream? In waking?

3. What would you think about yourself if other people saw you speaking or expressing yourself the same way in waking as you do in this dream?

4. Are there more things you would like to say or communicate in the dream but hold in for different reasons? In waking? List them:

a) _____
b) _____
c) _____
d) _____

These questions may force you to think more deeply about some of the ways that you communicate and express yourself in your dreams. You may find that you tend to ignore communication issues and just watch as life passes you by. You may feel shy and not know what to say in a situation, or you may not want to disturb the status quo in your family or at work. You may feel that not speaking up is safe, even when it may be holding you back from your full potential. When you aren't able to speak up, communicate, or express yourself to others, you may miss out on important relationships that can help you feel good and experience true connection.

It may take some time to make these changes. It is likely that you have developed a particular communication style over a long period of time, and that may be the only way you know how to express yourself. Learning how to notice some of these communication issues can help you to make changes later on.

Dream Opportunity Question

There is one more question that you can ask yourself to help you to get the most from this Dream Opportunity:

Do you believe you can speak up or express yourself more than you do in this dream?

This is a deep question that invites you to take a deeper look into your dreams. If you believe that you can use more expression or speak up more in your dreams, then can consider how you might do this. In the past, you may have behaved a certain way in the dream and never questioned it, because you were used to it. Now that you've practiced with the exercises in this section, you may realize that there is so much more you can do with your dreams, and so much more expression you can engage in.

Dream Opportunity Day

Sometime soon, take a Dream Opportunity Day. Make up an exercise that you think would help you have the dreams you want. Previously, you followed the Dreamosophy exercises. On this day, be inventive and make up your own. It can be anything. The kind of exercise is less important than doing it, because it is the doing that really helps you pay attention to your dreams.

It's not necessary to merely sit back and be an observer in the dreams you have. Being completely passive is often not ideal because it allows you to be controlled by others. There are many times when you have no control over the things that go on in your life, but your dreams need not be one of them. As you notice the dreams and your expressions within the dreams, you may start to feel unsatisfied with some of the responses you are giving. This chapter can help you to make changes that increase your power and satisfaction.

During the first level of this chapter, you've begun to look at your dreams in a new way. At this point, it can be helpful to teach someone else what you've just learned. This can reinforce what you are learning and can bring up new insights that may help you focus more on what you are doing. It may also make it easier for you to start speaking up in your dreams.

During this first week or so, you don't have to do much. It is not about understanding your dreams or even trying to interpret them or make them significant. Right now, you are just being invited to notice the different ways that you express yourself in your dreams, rather than trying to change them.

The longer you take to explore and practice at this level, the deeper and more profound your experience can be. This doesn't mean that you need to spend months working on this process, but it can be helpful to invest a little time on more than one or two days. Experiment with the dreams and invest the amount of time that you are comfortable with, to fully understand what kinds of expressions occur in your dreams.

Before moving on to the next level, take a look back and review all that you have learned in this first section. The opportunity to speak up in your dreams is important, but it can be equally important in your waking life! It's important to notice how much noise you make in your dreams, whether you make a little or a lot, as well as notice some of the different ways that you express yourself in your dreams. These are often connected to what you say and how you express yourself when you are awake. Take some time to think about how this opportunity, the Dream Opportunity of speaking up, is involved in all the aspects of your life!

SPEAK UP IN YOUR DREAMS! LEVEL TWO

Now that you have invested some time noticing your personal expression in your dreams, you may begin to notice some patterns. You may notice that you don't speak up and you don't express yourself in your dreams. You may just be someone who is there, waiting for someone else to tell you what to do at the different stages of your dream. This may relate to how you communicate and express yourself in real life. On the other hand, you may notice that you have an incredible amount of influence over what is going on in your dreams. You may notice that you have a lot of things to say in your dreams and that you express yourself in many different ways. Most people end up falling somewhere in between these two extremes.

During the first level, you invested time and attention noticing how you speak up in your dreams. As you did so, you may have made some connections between how you communicate in your dream life and in your waking life. You may have noticed a few changes that occurred in your level of dream communication as time went on. Now, you can move on to the second level.

In the second level, you will have the opportunity to move on from simply noticing what communication goes on in your dreams to actively identifying that communication, extending your knowledge a bit more. You may want to invest some time rating your dreams and comparing how much communication you have in your dreams to how much you have when you are awake. Let's look at what you can do to complete Level 2 of speaking up in your dreams.

Start by identifying your expressiveness. Remember that when you are looking for expressiveness in the dream, you are paying attention to how much noise and expression you make. This can include the things that you say, the way that you interact with other people, and the actions that you take in the dream. Here, you can use a scale to rate how much you speak up or express yourself in your dreams.

To begin identifying, start by GRAPHING your expressiveness. Remember, we are talking about making noise or communicating in any way. Use this scale to rate how much you speak up or express yourself.

Generally, taking all of your dreams into consideration, how much do you speak up or express yourself in your dreams?

1. NOT AT ALL: No outward expression of any of your thoughts or feelings in the dream.
2. SLIGHT: Some expression, but it is a minor feature of the dream.
3. MODERATE: Definite, but not effective expression.
4. STRONG: Your words, noises, and other forms of expression take preference over all your other activities, but are not central to the dream.
5. INTENSE: Prolonged and complete expression of your thoughts and feelings. Your words, sounds, and other expressions are a central aspect of the dream, even in the face of obstacles.

Next to your notes about this dream, write the number that corresponds to your general level of how much you speak up or express yourself in your dream life generally. GENERAL EXPRESSIVENESS: 1, 2, 3, 4, or 5.

Also next to your notes about this dream, write the number that corresponds to how much how much you speak up or express yourself in this dream. RECENT DREAM EXPRESSIVENESS: 1, 2, 3, 4, or 5.

While you are taking notes on the dream that you want to use, write down the number from above that corresponds to your general level of how much you speak or express yourself in the dream. There are no right or wrong answers in this part, so don't feel bad if your dreams score more or less than you think they 'should.' This doesn't mean that something is wrong with the way that you are dreaming; it just shows you what you may want to explore later on.

Past Questions

1. Using the 1-to-5 scale given earlier, on a new sheet or page of paper, write the number for your waking activity that best indicates how much you spoke up during the following periods of your life:

1 - 5 years old
6 - 12 years old
13 - 16 years old
17 - 21 years old
22 - 25 years old
26 - 35 years old
36 - 45 years old
46 - 55 years old
56 - 65 years old
66 - 75 years old
76 years and older

2. Now draw vertical and horizontal lines and numbers to create this graph of your level of expressiveness for each period of your life. Place a dot above each age; then connect the dots.

```
5


4


3


2


1
     _____
     age    1    6   13   17   22   26   36   46   56   66   76
```

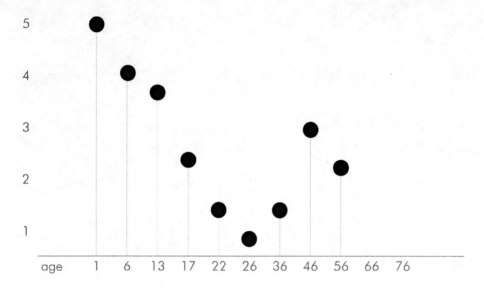

Your completed graph might look something like this after you connect the dots:

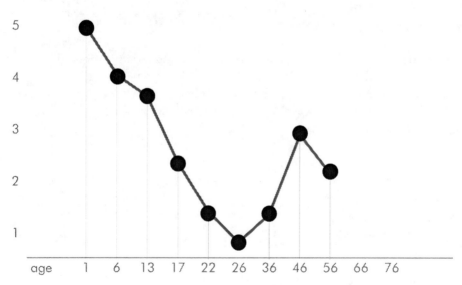

- Now look at the graph. Print it out if you can.
- Notice if your willingness and ability to speak up has changed over the years.
- Think about what has happened to you, how you have changed.

3. Think about how your parents, your friends, and your neighborhood may have determined your ability to speak up in your life.

4. Are you satisfied with how much you speak up and/or express yourself in your waking life?

5. List what kinds of expression were allowed as you were growing up, and what kinds were frowned upon.

ALLOWED:

a._____

b._____

c._____

FROWNED UPON:

a._____

b._____

c._____

Now, look at the graph. Do you notice that there are some changes in your willingness and your ability to speak up over time as things changed? Think about what has happened to you, how you have changed over the years, and how this affects how much you are willing to communicate and express yourself in your waking life.

These questions can help you to focus on what is going on in your life in terms of communication and how these could be influencing the communication that you have in your dreams. When you question your happiness with your current communication and your ability to speak up, you are more likely to want to make changes. This may be as beneficial to your dream life as it is to your waking life.

Dream Opportunity Question

Do you notice when other people really want to speak up more but hold back? What do you think, when you see them do it?

Whether or not you know it, you have been asked to think about things that most people try to avoid. Often people blame themselves for being a certain way without ever realizing that they were forced to be that way as they grew up and that now, if they could understand their Dream Opportunities, they could change.

Many people may find it frustrating when others want to speak up but hold back for some reason. If you know such people in your own life, you may feel bad for them and wish they could find the courage to speak out. You may wish to offer some advice on how to speak out and make a difference, but in the end, they have to be the ones to make that first step to see results.

If you are the person that has trouble speaking up, it can be very difficult. You may want to speak up, but there is something that keeps holding you back no matter how hard you try. Others may give you advice and you may realize that you really can step it up and make a difference with your expression and communication; but that knowledge may not seem to make a difference.

For those who don't tend to express themselves in real life, you are going to be invited to ask, why? Why are you holding back? Is it because you are too shy to speak up or you are scared of how others are going to view you, if you speak up about the things that you want? Some people don't want to rock the boat, while others worry about getting embarrassed. There are so many reasons why people may not want to speak up about something. Many reasons are valid – sometimes it's just not appropriate or not safe to speak up. So in those times, don't speak up, when you are awake. But is that really necessary in your dreams? What would happen, if you speak up just a little more, in your dreams? Now might be a good time to consider why you are not speaking up and communicating the way that you could, in your dreams. If you have solid reasons for nor speaking up when you are awake, do those same reasons really apply, when you are dreaming?

Bonus Exercises

Past: In any of your dreams, identify and list the ways in the dreams that you felt, acted, and thought that were the way you were as a child.

Present: Try to identify in your most recent dream a single way of talking, feeling, acting, or understanding that is completely yours the way you are now.

Future: Consider how you could have changed or completed your most recent dream:

- How could you have changed how much you spoke up?
- How could you have changed your level of understanding?
- How could you have changed the level of contact you had with other people in the dream?
- How could you have changed the actions you used in the dream?
- How could you have changed your level of feeling?

It may be most helpful to focus your energy on the future part of these exercises. This is the part where you can imagine how you would change your dreams and how you would make a difference so that your communication and expression are at a level that works for you. What would you need to do to speak up in the dream and really make yourself heard? Perhaps even re-imagine the dream with these changes to see how they feel.

While in Level 1 you focused on noticing how much you speak up in your dreams, Level 2 is a bit more interactive. You are invited to identify how much you speak up in the dream and how that relates to your life. Are there connections between the two, or is there a disconnect? Once you see how your dream and waking lives go together, it may be easier to move on to Level 3 and make some of the changes that you want in both your waking life and your dream life.

SPEAK UP IN YOUR DREAMS! LEVEL THREE

So far, this chapter has discussed how to notice and how to identify the ways that you speak up in your dream life and in your waking life. Level 3 takes this a step further as you explore transforming yourself yet again. Remember that you will be invited during this section to defy some of your own personal limits. Some of the tasks may seem simple for you to work with, while others may be more challenging than you expected.

In this level, you are going to be asked to introduce your Dream Opportunities into your waking life. If you are unwilling to try out something new in your waking time, you may find that all the progress you have seen so far in this Opportunity completely stops. This is just one reason why it can be important to step out of your comfort zone and try something new.

Of course, you can still be gentle with yourself. There is no race to get this level finished. Simply make an authentic effort and take as long as you feel you need. Just remember that you are the one in control of your results. You are invited to give the activities in this level your best effort, as this is the most likely to produce the results you desire. Skipping out on parts or rushing through activities can interfere with the unfolding process of Dreamosophy. So don't rush. There's nothing wrong with working at your own pace and doing what is comfortable for you.

Now we're going to invite you to bring this Dream Opportunity into your real life! To get started, pick a recent dream or make one up. Answer the following questions for each dream over the next week:

1. Are you satisfied with the way you speak up in this dream?
2. What would have to happen in this dream so that you could be totally satisfied with the way you speak up in the dream?
3. What is your main way of expressing yourself in this dream?
4. How do you keep yourself from speaking up as much as you would like?
5. What would you have to do or what would have to change, for you to fully express what you have to say?
6. Does the way you speak up in this dream work for you or against you?
7. How would you have to change the way you speak up to flow through to a whole new level?
8. Rate the way you speak up in this dream using the 1 to 5 scale given in Level 2. Generally, taking all of your dreams into consideration, how much do you speak up or express yourself in your dreams?

    1. NOT AT ALL: No outward expression of any of your thoughts or feelings in the dream.
    2. SLIGHT: Some expression, but it is a minor feature of the dream.
    3. MODERATE: Definite, but not effective expression.
    4. STRONG: Your words, noises, and other forms of expression take preference over all your other activities, but are not central to the dream.
    5. INTENSE: Prolonged and complete expression of your thoughts and feelings. Your words, sounds, and other expressions are a central aspect of the dream, even in the face of obstacles.

    What would it be like if you took your level of expression one level higher?
    What would it be like if you took your level of expression one level lower?

9. What good things might happen if you began to speak up as much as you would like to in your life?

Asking these questions is a good way to get started with speaking up more in your dreams. They can help you to realize where you are right now with your dreams and can help you to start seeing different ways you might want to speak up around others or in your dreams. It may be easier to work towards making some changes once you have this understanding.

Remember, with this part of the opportunity, you are going to bring together all the dreams you have over a certain amount of time and then rate them on this scale. There may be some dreams that have more activity and expression, and then there may be some dreams where you barely do any expressing at all. The idea is to get a good average to help you determine what steps to take next.

Take some time as you consider what would happen if things changed. For example, what would it be like for your dreams if you were able to take your level of speaking up one or two more levels? Most people are going to start on one of the lower levels, maybe at a two or a three, so how would it feel if you were able to get up to a four? Also, what would it feel like if you took your level of speaking and dropped it down another level? It's likely that you will enjoy how it feels to think about moving things up a level, but may find it less enjoyable to think about going down a level. This can be your motivation to learn how to speak up a bit more rather than being a bystander to the whole event.

Finding Your Dream Expressiveness Word

Write the ten main words you could use to describe what is happening in this dream.

1. _____
2. _____
3. _____
4. _____
5. _____
6. _____
7. _____
8. _____
9. _____
10. _____

Circle five of the words on your list of ten.

From the five circled words, write three on a new page.

1. _____
2. _____
3. _____

Of the three words, circle two.

From the two circled words, write one on a blank page, all by itself. That single word is your Dream Expressiveness Word. Remember your Dream Expressiveness Word throughout the day.

Waking Suggestion

Consider changing the way you speak up today. As you notice how you speak up, consider what it would be like to lessen it a little and then increase it. Try this out all day long, imagine what it would be like to lessen it a little and then increase it. NOTE: You may not actually change WHAT you say, perhaps just how much noise you make or how intensely you express yourself. Be respectful and responsible in all your actions in waking life. Be kind. Do not harm yourself or others in any way.

For the first day, you may want to change around the way that you speak up. Any time that you see an opportunity to speak up, consider taking it. As you notice how you are speaking up, try to first lessen it a little bit and then try to increase it again. Invest a little time doing this throughout the day, lessening how much you speak up in some instances and raising it in other areas. Make sure that you aren't trying to change what you want to say, just how much noise you are making or how intensely you are expressing yourself.

During this time, you are exploring getting more influence over how much you express yourself. Often, you may get pushed to the side and only speak up when others want you to behave in a certain way. You get to decide how much and in what manner you would like to express yourself. This doesn't mean that you should make fun of others or be mean and cruel or say things that will get you in trouble. It just means that you may be able to find a manner to express yourself and let it shine — a way that is uniquely and artfully yours, without worrying too much about what other people say.

You may find that you have trouble with this. Speaking up can be uncomfortable and unfamiliar for a lot of people. Do not be imprudent — don't do anything drastic, that might get you in trouble. If you feel that you are doing something wrong by behaving in this manner, don't do it — just imagine what it would be like. Remember, this approach is about your DREAM life. But to see success, you might consider giving it a try. It doesn't have to be a crazy big thing, but imagining what it would be like to speak up on a few things during the day can help you to get out of your comfort zone a little bit and start building up more confidence, in ways that may show up in your dream life. If you notice that you weren't able to express yourself more, or that you didn't feel comfortable doing so, that's okay — but just notice, what were the things that stopped you? Did you feel less active? Did you get confused? Did you restrict your ability to feel good? It may take a few days to try this out, but eventually, speaking out and expressing yourself can come more naturally and you can learn to do it without thinking so much.

Even if you just begin to imagine what it would be like to speak up more in your waking life, this will start to translate into your dream life as well. You will be able to express yourself more in your dreams and you can influence the way that you speak up in your dreams, without having to sit on the side and hope that others will do something you like in the dream. Dreaming can be so much more enjoyable when you get to speak up, direct the show, and enjoy the different ways that you can express yourself.

Maintaining the Changes

Learning how to speak up and express yourself more in your waking life and in your dream life is a big deal. It can truly help you gain some of the confidence you may be looking for. You may have already noticed that your dreams have begun to change as you've engaged with the exercises in Levels 1, 2, and 3. The next step is to keep that momentum going. Maintaining your progress is important, so that you can maintain your influence over the things you do in your dreams.

If you have done the exercises in Levels 1, 2, and 3, your dreams have probably begun to change already. Here is a series of questions you can use to maintain the changes.
1. How did you like the way you expressed yourself in this dream?
2. What is the dream trying to tell you about your waking life?
3. What is this dream trying to tell you about your future?
4. How can you change your opportunity so that the present and future circumstances in the story work for you?

If you are not satisfied with how you speak up in your dreams, repeat the exercises in Level 3 on a different day, with a different dream. If you are still not satisfied, repeat them again, on yet another day. You can also return to the exercises in Levels 1 and 2, for greater insight and sensitivity. Keep repeating, until your dreams provide additional insight and guidance.

Bonus Exercise

Now that you have gone through this Dream Opportunity, you are going to be invited to explore a few bonus exercises! These exercises are great for helping you to think about how you would like to see yourself in the future and what aspirations you would prefer in your life. For the first part, take out a pen and paper and list out all the changes you want to have in your life for the next year. It doesn't matter what the goals or aspirations are, just write and perhaps add in a few ideas of how you might get this done, if you have any ideas about that.

Keep this list in a location where you can see it each day. This can help to give you a little bit more motivation for realizing your fondest dreams, and when you see how well you are moving towards these dreams, your confidence can increase. You may also want to take some time each month and revise the list to reflect aspirations that you accomplish or new ones that you want to achieve.

IN SUMMARY

Speaking up in your dreams is something that can take time and attention to accomplish. Most people are not used to the idea that they can express themselves and speak up in their dreams because it seems like a lot of hard work. They may have trouble expressing themselves in their waking lives, so they are uncertain about how to express themselves in their dream lives as well.

This chapter is all about learning how to speak up in your dreams and in your waking life. It can be really frustrating to go through life and not have any influence over what is going on. Many times, in both your waking and dream lives, you may end up letting someone else take center stage. You may go along with what others do and say, perhaps even when that isn't a true expression of who you are. Learning how to express yourself and speak out more in your real life and in your dream life can help to change this and give you a new sense of happiness that you may have missed out on in the past.

Levels 1 and 2 of this opportunity concentrated on noticing how you speak up and how you express yourself in your dreams. For some, realizing that not much expression is happening in the dream world – or even in real life - can be difficult. However, this is not necessarily a bad thing even if your dream expressions are close to non-existent. It's simply something that can be helpful to explore over time.

You may not get as much as is possible out of your dreams until you are able to experience them as an opportunity to speak up and to express yourself. Dreams are great places to express yourself because there really isn't anyone there to judge or make fun of you. If you aren't able to speak up and find new and creative ways to express yourself in your dreams, then how will you be able to do the same when you are awake?

The good news is that you can learn to have some influence with all this, and that will come as you continue to explore the exercises in Level 3. During that level, you learned how you could make some changes in the amount of expression that you are able to use. Yes, this does mean that you can speak up and talk with other people, perhaps making it an aspiration to have one meaningful conversation a day; but there are other methods of expressing yourself if you find the conversation stuff a bit too much. For example, you can express yourself in writing, dancing, exercising, poetry, cooking, and more. The idea is to find the method of expressing yourself that works for you and then stick with it, or keep trying alternatives, until you see results.

Many times, it is easy to get pushed to the side and feel like you aren't influencing your own destiny, because so many other people are taking over for you. But when you use your talents and start speaking up and expressing yourself, you may discover that it's easier than ever to benefit from the human capacity to express and communicate.

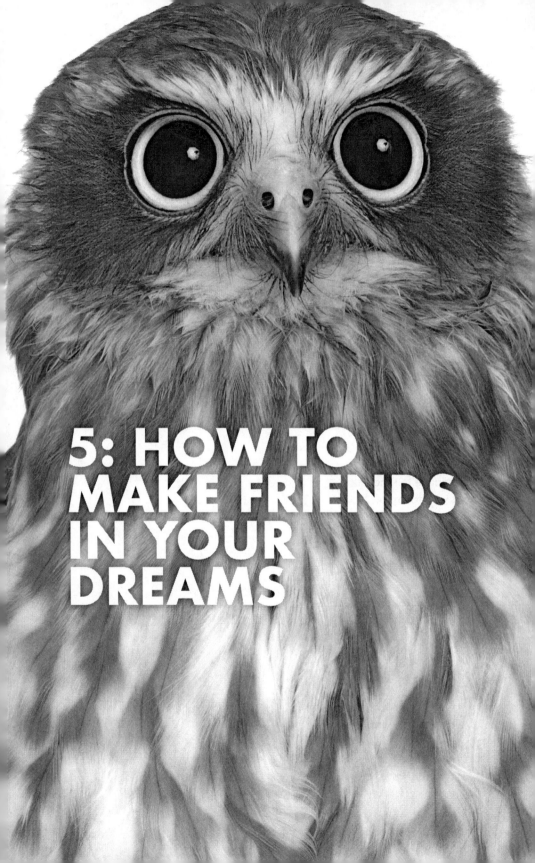

5: HOW TO MAKE FRIENDS IN YOUR DREAMS

In this chapter, you will be invited to learn about making friends in your dreams. This is an exciting Dream Opportunity offering a skill that a lot of people don't realize they are able to enjoy in their dreams. As with some of the other Dream Opportunities in this guidebook, many individuals feel that they have no influence over what goes on in their dreams. They may just be reliving something that happened during the day or acting as innocent bystanders, going along for the ride with no other choices.

But in your dream, you can influence so many things. You can decide how much freedom and influence you have in your actions during the dream, you can influence how much feeling you have in the dream, and you can even figure out how to speak up and express yourself more in the dream. All these are connected to the interactions you have in your waking life, so learning how to add more control, feelings, and expression into your daily life can help you get more of these in your dreams as well.

Another experience that you may be able to find in your dreams is the ability to make new friends. Think of how exciting it would be to go to sleep at night and know that you are able to make a few new friends! During your dreaming, you may have noticed that there were other people present, some of whom may have had part to play in the dream and others who were in the background. You may have felt that, while all these people are near you, you weren't able to interact with them.

Exploring this Dream Opportunity can help you learn how to meet some of the people in your dreams. You can pick and choose the people that you want to talk with in your dream and even how you would like to interact with them. You can pick out the person who is the most important in the dream and interact with them, or you can just pick a random person in the dream and begin a conversation. You can participate in your dream. You might be amazed by all the cool people you get to learn about and interact with.

This chapter will invite you to invest some time discussing how you can make some friends in your dreams. You can choose to make some new friends each time you go to sleep, or you can bring up the same people in more than one dream so that you are able to meet your friends again each time you wade into the dreamstream. This is a great way to enjoy your dreams more, gain insights while you are sleeping, and so much more. Let's get started learning how to use this Dream Opportunity to meet new people while you are asleep.

MAKE FRIENDS IN YOUR DREAMS! LEVEL ONE

As with other Dream Opportunities, the first level of this Dream Opportunity is to notice what is going on in your dreams. During this part, you will just be invited to take some time to look over the dreams that you are having and notice how you are interacting with other people in your dreams. And also as with the other Dream Opportunities, it's important to make sure that you remember your dreams. If you have not mastered the art of remembering your dreams, you may wish to go back to the first chapter and practice the steps for remembering your dreams before moving forward.

This level is all about noticing what's going on in your dreams. You don't need to put a lot of effort into the dreams that you have. As long as you are already able to remember your dreams, you've finished the hard part of this process! From here, you can simply go to bed and try to take notice of the interactions that you have with others in your dreams. You will explore identifying and making changes to your dream interactions later, but for right now, simply notice the things that you do in your dreams.

This level works best if you can track your dreams for a week or two, based on how deeply you have decided to explore, as you move through the exercises. You might choose to write down some notes about the dreams to help you remember them later, and then answer the questions in the following activities all at once. Or, you can choose to do these activities with each dream right away in the mornings, before you get up and go on with your day.

For each dream, ask yourself the following questions:

1. How much contact did you have with others in this dream?

2. What is your main way of making contact?

3. Did you move towards others in the dream?

4. Did you actually touch others?

5. Did you have emotional contact?
   That is, did you have any feelings towards others in the dream?

6. Did other dream characters have emotional contact with you?

7. List all the different ways of making contact physically or emotionally in the dream, the most important first:

a._____
b._____
c._____
d._____

8. In the dream overall, did you tend to move toward or away from other characters or aspects of the dream?

9. Were others in this dream known to you?

a. Were they strangers?
b. Were there more strangers?
c. Were there more people you knew?

These questions invite you to notice what is going on in your dream. You may bring up that first dream and notice that you aren't able to answer some of these questions. You may not have had any interaction with the people in the dream, whether it was physical or emotional interaction, or you may not even remember who was in the dream. Don't feel discouraged. These questions can help you to think about what's going on in the dream, and then you can work harder in the next dream to try to notice what's going on around you with the people in your dream.

Remember that during this step you are not trying to change things in your dream world. This level is all about noticing your interactions in your dreams. Later, you can explore making some changes.

Waking Questions

Once you are done asking yourself the questions above, you can move on to your waking life. It's likely that you will find some connections between the personal interactions that you have in your dreams and the ones that you have in your waking life. Ask yourself the following questions:

1. How much contact do you have with others in your waking life?

2. Do you tend to avoid or move toward emotional contact with others?

3. Do you have more contact with strangers or people you know already?

4. How often do you actually touch others?

5. How often do others touch you?

As you answer these questions, take some time to think about how your answers compare to what you felt and saw in your dream. You aren't working to make any changes at this point, but notice the connections that are showing up in your dreams and how they relate to what is going on in your waking life. Are you happy with the interactions that you have in your personal life, or do you feel they are lacking? If they are lacking, what is the main reason? Later, you will explore making some changes to your social interactions, but this level just focuses on noticing your interactions so you can explore them later!

Dream Opportunity Question

Would you prefer to have more or less contact with others than you do in this dream?

Dream Opportunity Day

When you have a chance, take a Dream Opportunity Day. As with previous Dream Opportunities, you can simply make up any kind of exercise to help you have the dreams that you want. You will create a dream exercise for yourself, instead of using only the dream exercises that were provided in this chapter. The aspiration for this exercise is to influence the number or type of interactions you have in your dreams.

The type of exercise that you come up with is not that important. You can get creative and make it whatever you would like. For this exercise, it is more important to come up with something and do it, than to concentrate on what type of exercise it is. The process of creating and carrying out the exercise can help you to pay better attention to your dreams, regardless of the activity.

MAKE FRIENDS IN YOUR DREAMS! LEVEL TWO

Now that you've begun to realize how much you interact with other people in your dream life and in your waking life, whenever you're ready, you can to move on to Level 2. In this level, you will invest some time identifying the contact you have with others, and even identifying some of the reasons that you behave in a certain way. You will be able to put some of this information into a graph to help you to understand what is going on in your dreams and in your daily life.

In this step, you are still not making changes. Instead, you are defining how much contact you have with others. This can be very important for helping you to understand what is going on in your life when it comes to social interactions, and it can make it easier to figure out where things might or might not consider the possibilities for change.

This is a very important step toward making changes in your social life. You may begin to realize that the amount of social interaction you have in your dreams is related to how much social interaction you have when you are awake. Humans are naturally social beings, so when they aren't able to socialize with others much or they have trouble interacting, it could be a sign of a problem. Yes, there are introverts who tend to recharge by being at home and not socializing as often, but even these individuals still want to get out there and socialize with their peers on occasion. Luckily, there are some steps you can take to change your social interaction level, and Level 2 is the first step to making that happen.

To begin this level, start by graphing out how much contact you currently have with others in your dreams. There is no right or wrong answer, so be honest during this phase so you have an idea of your starting point. Over time, you may notice that your interactions increase in your dreams and your rating scale gets higher. But, for now, there is nothing wrong with picking a lower number. The important thing is to be as accurate as possible.

To get started with this part, you are invited to either pick a recent dream, or think back to any of the recent dreams you can remember. When you take these dreams into consideration, determine how much contact you seem to have with others in your dreams, using the following scale.

To begin identifying, start by GRAPHING how much contact you have with others. Remember, we are talking about making contact in any way. Use this scale to rate your level of contact.

Generally, taking all of your dreams into consideration, how much contact do you have with others in your dreams?

1. NO CONTACT: You are present in the dream only as an observer.
2. SLIGHT AND OCCASIONAL: Your contact with others is indirect, and does not affect the actions or feelings of the dream.
3. MODERATE: You speak with others and have emotional contact, but you often avoid or move away from the contacts.
4. SOLID AND DIRECT: Your contacts with others are solid and direct, often physical, and they do affect the outcome of the dream.
5. TOTAL: Your contacts with others are complete, intense, fulfilling, involving deep feelings. Your contact with others is central to the dream and makes a difference.

Next to your notes about this dream, write the number that corresponds to your general level of contact with others in your dream life generally. GENERAL CONTACT: 1, 2, 3, 4, or 5.

Also next to your notes about this dream, write the number that corresponds to how much contact you have in this dream. RECENT DREAM CONTACT: 1, 2, 3, 4, or 5.

Past Questions

The next step is to look at your past and determine how much contact you have had with other people throughout the different phases of your life. This will get you thinking about how much your social interactions have changed over the years, and what this could mean for your dream time.

1. Using the 1-to-5 scale, on new sheet or page of paper, write the number for your level of contact when you are awake that indicates the level of contact you had during the following periods of your life:

1 - 5 years old	22 - 25 years old	56 - 65 years old
6 - 12 years old	26 - 35 years old	66 - 75 years old
13 - 16 years old	36 - 45 years old	76 years and older
17 - 21 years old	46 - 55 years old	

2. Now draw vertical and horizontal lines and numbers to create this graph of your level of contact for each period of your life. Place a dot above each age, then connect the dots.

5

4

3

2

1

age   1   6   13   17   22   26   36   46   56   66   76

Your distribution of dots might look something like this:

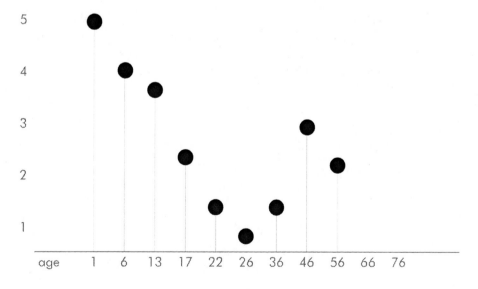

Your completed graph might look something like this after you connect the dots:

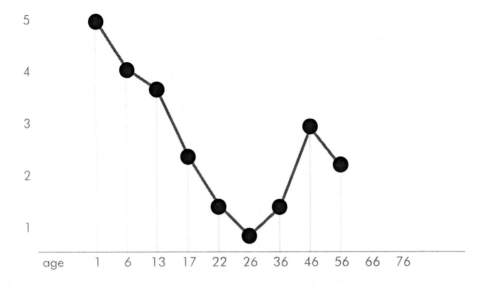

- Now look at the graph. Print it out if you can.
- Notice if your level of contact has changed over the years.
- Think about what has happened to you, how you have changed.

3. Think about how your parents, your friends, and your neighborhood may have determined your willingness to make contact with others in your life.

4. Are you satisfied with the level of contact and friendship you have in your waking life?

5. List what types of contact you were allowed as you were growing up, and what kinds were frowned upon.

ALLOWED:

a._____

b._____

c._____

FROWNED UPON:

a._____

b._____

c._____

You may notice that your level of social interaction does change over the years, but each person will be different. Some people may have more social interactions as they get older, while others may see a drop in interactions as they get older. At this point, just assign a number for each age group, and don't worry about the rest.

During this time, you can think about the people in your life and how they have influenced you. Oftentimes, the amount of social interactions you have depends on how you were raised and the interactions you had as a child. In other instances, there may have been a big event that changed the way you interact with others. Take some time to consider how your parents, your friends, and your neighbors may have determined your willingness to make contact with others in your life.

Take a moment to consider how satisfied you are with your current level of contact and friendship with others in your waking life. Some people may be really social and feel that they need to have more contact with other people, but there is something in their way that is preventing them from getting as much contact as they would like. Then, there are those who don't like as much contact, who like to be on their own, and they may be fine with the amount of contact they currently have, even if the amount is low, by comparison. The answer to this will vary based on your current situation and what you enjoy and feel most comfortable with.

Dream Opportunity Question

Do you notice when other people have opportunities to make friendly contacts but don't? What do you think to yourself, when this happens?

This exercise can help you see how many times you have an opportunity to make contact with others and how many times you skip out on them. Many times, you may have opportunities to be social and make contact, but may ignore those opportunities or not even notice that they exist. In this exercise, think critically about the questions that are asked and try to see why you act in a certain way.

Do you notice when other people have an opportunity to make friendly contacts, but you aren't able to make these contacts? What are the thoughts that you think to yourself when this happens? Are you upset that you are not able to make any of these connections, or do you get jealous? Or, are you someone who is happy with the social interactions that you have, and so you feel happy that the other person made a new connection? Are you willing to go out of your comfort zone and actually make that social connection and friendly contact work for you?

Whether you realize it or not, this section has asked you to think about a lot of things that might be a bit uncomfortable. These are often things that people want to avoid. Often, people blame themselves for behaving in a certain way, without realizing that they were taught how to be this way when they were growing up. The good news is that if you understand your Dream Opportunities, you can make changes.

Bonus Exercises

Before you move on to Level 3, here are a few bonus exercises for the second level. These questions are going to ask you to look at your past, present, and future to determine how you have changed your thoughts and feelings over time, starting with your childhood and ending with how you would like to do things in the future. This can be a good way to get you thinking about how your current social interaction level matches up with how you were taught to behave. The extra exercises that you can do to finish the second level include the following:

Past: In any of your dreams, identify and list the ways in the dreams that you felt, acted, and thought that were the way you were as a child.

Present: Try to identify in your most recent dream a single way of talking, feeling, acting, or understanding that is completely yours the way you are now.

Future: Consider how you could have changed or completed your most recent dream:
- How could you have changed the level of contact you had with other people in the dream?
- How could you have changed how much you spoke up?
- How could you have changed your level of understanding?
- How could you have changed the actions you used in the dream?
- How could you have changed your level of feeling?

In Level 1 and Level 2, you took a little time to notice and identify what is going on in your dreams. This is a great way to learn how much contact you have with other people in your dreams, and you can determine if you are satisfied with the level of interaction. You may consider your dreams and notice that the interaction is pretty high or that you are satisfied with it even though the amount is low. On the other hand, there are some people who will notice that the levels are low and may want to make changes. The first two levels are just about realizing how much interaction is going on in your dreams and in your waking life, before moving on to the third level and putting these realizations into action.

MAKE FRIENDS IN YOUR DREAMS! LEVEL THREE

During the first two levels, you learned how to notice and identify the different connections you made in your dream life and in your waking life. You took the time to chart the connections that you had in your dream life. In some instances, you may have been happy with the results, while at other times you may have been surprised at the lack of connections you were having. In some instances, you may have just been an onlooker, without having any interactions or doing anything active, while at other times, you may have gotten a chance to interact and even physically touch other people in the dream. It all depends on your connection in the dreams and how you interact with people outside your dreams.

In this third level, you will move on and start making some changes to the way that you interact with other people. So far, you've invested time recognizing the amount of contact that you have with other people in your dreams and in your waking life. Now, you can move on to making a change. Some people may notice that the level of contact and relationship with others around them, whether they are looking at their dreams or their waking life, is pretty low. In Level 3 of this Dream Opportunity, you can move on to learning how you can change the amount and quality of your relationships.

To start this part, recall one of your most recent dreams. You may find that it is helpful to go with your most recent dream each day for a week, so that you can really focus on these questions and determine what is going on in each of the dreams. Once you have the dream ready with a few written notes, you can answer the following questions:

1. Are you satisfied with your level of friendship in this dream?
2. What would have to happen in this dream for you to be friends with everyone in the dream?

3. Who is your best friend in this dream?
4. How do you avoid contact with others in the dream?
5. What would you have to do or what would have to change, to make friends in the dream?
6. Does the level of friendship in this dream work for you or against you?
7. How would you have to change your level of contact to flow through to a whole new level?
8. Rate the way you make contact in this dream using the 1 to 5 scale given in Level 2.

Generally, taking all of your dreams into consideration, how much contact do you have with others in your dreams?

1. NO CONTACT: You are present in the dream only as an observer.
2. SLIGHT AND OCCASIONAL: Your contact with others is indirect, and does not affect the actions or feelings of the dream.
3. MODERATE: You speak with others and have emotional contact, but you often avoid or move away from the contacts.
4. SOLID AND DIRECT: Your contacts with others are solid and direct, often physical, and they do affect the outcome of the dream.
5. TOTAL: Your contacts with others are complete, intense, fulfilling, involving deep feelings. Your contact with others is central to the dream and makes a difference.

What would it be like if you took your level of contact one level higher?
What would it be like if you took your level of contact one level lower?

9. What good things might happen if you began to have as much contact as you would like to in your life?

These questions are meant to get you thinking about how your interactions in your dreams are going. Sometimes, you will have a dream that has a lot of great interaction and contact between you and the other people in the dream, and then other times, you will have very little interaction going on. In the beginning, you may find that many of your dreams are low on interaction because you are so used to sitting on the sidelines and watching what is going on in the dream. But, the more that you question yourself about the interactions and relationships that you form in your dreams, the stronger they will get.

Keep in mind that there are no right or wrong answers. No one besides you will see the results, so be honest with yourself about what you write down. You can rate your dreams by combining all the dreams together to come up with an average, or do this each day for a week or two for each dream individually.

Many people who go through this part notice that there are limitations on the amount of contact they are having with other people, whether they are looking at their dream life or their waking life. One thing to consider is the good things that may happen if you began to have as much contact as you would like to in your life. What would it feel like if you were able to control when you met new people, if you were able to speak up and be around others even more, or if you had an easier time making new friends? Your level of contact with others may directly influence your quality of life. Understanding the amazing changes that can come from this can make a big difference.

Finding Your Dream Friendship Word

Write the ten main words you could use to describe what is happening in your dream.

1. _____
2. _____
3. _____
4. _____
5. _____
6. _____
7. _____
8. _____
9. _____
10. _____

Circle five of the words on your list of ten.

From the five circled words, write three on a new page.

1. _____
2. _____
3. _____

Of the three words, circle two.

From the two circled words, write one on a blank page, all by itself. That single word is your Dream Friendship Word. Remember your Dream Friendship Word throughout the day.

Waking Suggestion

Now that you have invested some time with the contacts in your dreams, you are cordially invited to bring some of this into your waking life. The first exercise invites you to try to change the way that you make contact with others. At first, just notice how much contact you are making during the day. You may notice that your contact is pretty limited in the beginning, but you are going to have some chances to increase or decrease the contact as you go along.

1. Try to change the way you make contact today. As you notice how you make contact, lessen it a little and then increase it. Be respectful and appropriate. Do not do anything illegal, improper, or harmful during waking life. Try this out all day long, lessen it a little and then increase it. Be respectful and responsible in all your actions in waking life. Do not harm yourself or others in any way.

2. Before you go on, did you really try out some of those new things? If not, at least notice and identify how you stopped yourself.

Did you get confused?
Less active?
Did you restrict your ability to feel good?
Did you speak up less?

Remember that it's important to be appropriate and respectful. Do not do anything that is harmful, improper, or illegal, to yourself or to others during your waking life. Always be responsible and respectful in all your actions in your waking life.

The neat thing about this is that you will be able to explore the level of friendship and interaction that you are having with other people in your waking life. There are so many interactions that are great for you, from ones that help you to build new friendships to those that will help you to network and make new acquaintances to further your career and get closer to your aspirations. Learning how to ease that contact up and down throughout the day may allow you to form the connections that you are looking for in your waking life more easily, as well.

It's important to do the activities in this chapter to see results. You may get better at forming connections with others in your waking life, but you may also consider navigating some of the insecurities and other less comfortable things that are getting in your way first. When you are able to move through some of those uncomfortable areas, even if it's just a little bit at a time (you can split this activity up into a few days or do it a few different times), you can form some meaningful relationships and connections that can be very satisfying.

Maintaining the Changes

For some people, this may be the hardest part. They may not be comfortable with talking to other people or speaking up so that they can meet other people. Others may be more comfortable and won't have an issue at all. Each person is different. Moving towards the aspiration of making more friends can make a huge difference in the long run. No matter how easy or hard this Dream Opportunity was for you, it is important that you maintain it, so that you can have solid friendships and resilient connections in all areas of your life.

If you have done the exercises in Levels 1, 2, and 3, your dreams have probably begun to change already. Here is a series of questions you can use to maintain the changes.

1. How friendly did you feel towards others in this dream?
2. What is the dream trying to tell you about your waking life?
3. What is this dream trying to tell you about your future?
4. How can you change your opportunity so that the present and future circumstances in the story work for you?

If you are not satisfied with how you make friends in your dreams, repeat the exercises in Level 3 on a different day, with a different dream. If you are still not satisfied, repeat them again, on yet another day. You can also return to the exercises in Levels 1 and 2, for greater insight and sensitivity.

Bonus Exercises

These extra exercises can help you learn more about yourself. They can also help you concentrate on the things that you want in the future. This is an opportunity to think about your short-term aspirations, such as the ones that you have for the next year. Here, you can list many of the changes that you aspire to in your life over time.

When this list is done, it can be helpful to take the time to review it each day. You can place it on the fridge or keep it somewhere else, where you will see it often. This is a great way to remind yourself to keep moving towards your aspirations. If you stick this list somewhere that you will forget about, it may be harder to remember these aspirations. Your fondest dreams are always there, but if you don't remember or attend to them, sometimes they remain just dreams, and never become real. Sometimes you might prefer to keep those fond dreams in the realm of fantasy – that's okay – but with other dreams, perhaps they are your true aspirations in life, and you would prefer to realize those dreams.

Each month, take some time to go through that list and see which things are still valid. For example, if you achieve an aspiration, you can check it off the list. If you end up wanting to add a new aspiration, you can to put it on the list so that you are able to remember it again. The list will likely change over time, but it is a good reminder to help you stay in the flow of dream realization – having your life become a dream come true.

By the end of Level 3, you have cultivated the chance to form different connections with others, both in your personal waking life and in your dreams. Your dreams may start becoming more powerful and even more fun, as you begin to choose the way that you would like to interact with those around you. Keep remembering through these different exercises to help bring dreams into manifestation.

IN SUMMARY

It is possible to make some new friends and have some great interactions in your dreams. While you may be used to just sitting back and watching the dreams that you have rather than associating with other people, you can use the suggestions in this chapter to help you to start meeting others who are in your dreams in no time. By learning how to add more interactions into your waking life, or at least control these interactions, you can help yourself make new friends in your dreams right from the beginning.

In the first level, you are responsible for just noticing what happens in your dreams. Whether you take each dream for a week and look through it one at a time or you try to average out your recent dreams, you can invest this time trying to see what connections are available and how you react to others in your dream. Very few people start out having good connections with others in their dreams, so you may notice some times when you withdraw from social situations in your dreams and you may just sit back and watch the dream without trying to associate with others at all. As you work through this Dream Opportunity, things may start to get easier and you may find that it is possible to meet new people and interact with others in your dreams.

As you move into Level 2, you may notice that your interactions with others in your dreams will correspond with the interactions that you have with others in your waking life. Are you someone who often withdraws from relationships with others, who doesn't speak up or worry about meeting someone new when they are at work or in social situations? If you are a withdrawn person who doesn't want to meet new people or who is shy about meeting them, you may find that your situation will be the same in your dreams.

In the second level, you invested some time exploring the different ways that you interact with others in your dream world and in your waking world. The two are often going to be very similar to each other so if you want to be able to change what is going on in your dream world, you might consider changing the way that you act in your waking life, as well. In this second level, you invested time identifying how you socialize with other people, not only in your dream world, but also in how you interact with others when you are awake. You did not work at making changes; you just invested this time noticing and identifying the things that were going on around you.

In the third level, you finally got to make change. In this level, you started to change how you interacted with others in your waking life. You made the effort to change how you interacted with other people in different situations. Sometimes, you added in more interaction and then at others times you added in less. This exercise was all about noticing how you interact with other people and learning how you are able to control how you interact with others. You can then use this knowledge to decide how much you would like to interact with others so you are still at a level that is comfortable for yourself.

When all this comes together, it is much easier to learn how to make more friends, in your personal life and in your dream life, which can be a great thing. You don't have to be friends with everyone you meet, but learning how to be more open to these friendships and what they can bring into your life, rather than letting your insecurities get in the way and holding you back, can make a big difference. If at any time you feel that this Dream Opportunity is not working well for you, make sure to go back through the levels again or invest more time on each level. Each person goes at their own pace. Learning how to make this work for you can really make a difference in how well you are able to form some good relationships in your life.

6: HOW TO UNDERSTAND AND REALIZE DREAMS

One thing that a lot of people like to explore with their dreams is learning how to understand what is going on in these dreams. They like the idea of thinking about things in their dreams and coming up with a solution, rather than worrying about them in their waking life. There are plenty of things that you can do to fully understand your dreams. This chapter will help you to get started.

There were several times in this guidebook where you worked to control and understand what your dreams were telling you. You worked on talking more in your dreams, making more friends, feeling good, and even gaining more freedom. You were able to understand that there was a connection between your waking life and your dream life. For example, if you have trouble making friends and talking to people in your dreams, it is often because you are experiencing these same troubles in your personal life. All the topics discussed in this guidebook can be related back to your personal life, which in turn may help you to better understand what is going on in your dreams.

There is so much that can be understood and realized in dreams. If you can remember your dreams, you can learn something. It all starts with simply noticing some of the things that happen in your dreams. When you first get started, it's easy to just think about the dream and not pay attention to what's going on. You may not even notice the details of the dream. But, if you would like to really understand what is going on in your dreams, you can take some time to notice a few of the details that are there, and then figure out how they relate to you personally in your daily life.

Each person is going to have a different outcome from this process. Your personal life is different from that of anyone else, and understanding your dreams will depend on some of your own personal experiences in your waking life. Talking to others about your dreams can help you to remember what you dreamt about, but don't invest too much time comparing your dreams to the dreams of other people. There is no right or wrong way to dream. Everyone will have different dreams, so it's most helpful to focus on yours and how you experience them rather than on other people's.

There are many instances of dreams working to help people understand what is going on in their lives. This chapter invites you to invest some time to understand your dreams in a way that you may never have imagined. Following the same template as the previous chapters, you will start by noticing what goes on in your dreams, then identifying, and finally making some changes that can help you truly understand what is going on in your dreams.

Let's get started!

UNDERSTAND AND REALIZE DREAMS! LEVEL ONE

This chapter will offer you a few different questions you can ask yourself to better understand what's going on in your dreams. This part is split up into several different sections, including questions about your dreams, waking questions about what goes on in your daily life, and the chance to explore a Dream Opportunity Day. These activities can help you to understand what is going on in your personal life and in your dreams.

During this first level, you will invest time noticing what happens in your dreams. You don't have to make any changes, yet. You are just responsible for noticing what is going on in your dreams so you can begin to understand them. To get the most out of this work, it's important to put in your best effort. Go at your own pace and go through the steps a few times each if needed, but try to avoid skipping parts of this Opportunity or rushing through. Otherwise, you may not see the results that you want.

To get started, remember one of your recent dreams, or make one up. Remember that you can do this multiple times, perhaps going through and doing it every day for a week or so, in order to help you understand what is going on in the dream and to help make this process a bit easier.

Once you have a dream ready, ask yourself the following questions to help you get started:

1. How clear is this dream?

   a. How vivid were the colors?

   b. Were the images fuzzy or a clear picture?

   c. Did you understand everything that happened when you woke up?

   d. Did the dream make sense to you when you were dreaming?

2. How clear were you as the dreamer?

3. Do you have a starring role or secondary part?

4. Do you like the way you are in this dream?

5. Are you participating in this dream or just observing?

6. What is the main activity in this dream?

7. List all the roles (ways of doing things, moving, or acting) in this dream:

a. _____
b. _____
c. _____
d. _____

Which one do you like the most?

8. List the characters in order of how well they understood what was going on in the dream:

a. _____
b. _____
c. _____
d. _____
e. _____

Your answers can never be right or wrong, so don't worry about what you are writing down. If you felt that there was another character in your dream that had more power and who understood what was going on in the dream better than you did, that's fine. You may be able to change that later on and gain more comprehension of your dreams. If you are you not happy with the role you were playing in the dream, you want to make some changes. As you move through this section, you can come to understand why you have certain roles in your dreams and even how you are able to change them later on.

Waking Questions

Now that you have had some time to go through one of your dreams and ask the questions above, here are some waking questions. These are questions that you can ask about your waking life. They can help you to draw some connections between your waking life and your dream life. Ask yourself the following:

1. How much do you understand what happens at work in your waking life?

2. How much do you understand what happens when you're at play?

3. How much to you understand what happens in your relationships?

4. Do you act on what you know?

5. Do you silently think about things?

6. Do things seem to just happen to you?

7. Do you know the cause and effect of what is going on in your life?

8. Do most other people in your life understand more than you do?

These are hard questions to answer about yourself. It's easy to go through the day feeling that you are doing just fine, but never looking at what is going on in your life. You may feel like you are always lost and confused or like you don't know what's going on in the world around you because you are so far behind. You may think it was just because you forgot some important things going on at work or at school, but often it is because you just don't understand what is going on in your life. These questions will help you to focus more on how much you really understand about your waking life so you can explore the possibilities of making change.

Body Questions

While you were dreaming, did you clearly see your body in the dream?

What parts, if any, were missing?

Take a moment to go back to the dream you were focusing on earlier. Think through it and get to the part where you are able to see yourself the most clearly. While you were dreaming, did you clearly see your body in the dream? Were you able to look at the dream, or look down at yourself while in the dream, and see parts of your body? There is nothing wrong with not being able to see your body at all during this phase, but if you did see your body, what parts, if any, were not there or were missing?

Being aware of yourself in the dream can be a big thing, so you may find that in some dreams, you were able to see your body well and other times you weren't. The more that you are able to see and recognize your own body in the dream, the more understanding and connection you are likely to have with your dreams.

Dream Opportunity Day

Sometime during the week, take a Dream Opportunity Day: Make up an exercise that you think would help you have the dreams you want. Previously, you followed the Dreamosophy exercises. On this day, be inventive and make up your own. It can be anything. The kind of exercise is less important than doing it, because it is the doing that really helps you pay attention to your dreams.

Once again, the exercise can be ANYTHING. If you want, you could sing a song while hopping up and down on one foot and that would be a good Dream Opportunity exercise. You'd probably remember it! Pick a day during the week, any day that works best for you, and create your own Dream Opportunity Day. On this day, it is your responsibility to make up an exercise that you think would help you to have the dreams that you want.

Make sure to be inventive and creative during this day. There are no right or wrong answers for this exercise, so you can just have some fun and come up with an activity that you think will be helpful, or at least enjoyable. It is more important for you to do the activity, no matter what it is, than to focus on the type of activity that you choose to explore. It's about engaging your awareness of dreaming by doing the activity in the first place.

Understanding what's going on in your dreams can take some time and practice to accomplish. Too many times, you have probably awakened from one of your dreams and been completely confused by what went on in that dream. Even during the dream, you may have been along for the ride without truly realizing what was happening to you while you slept. Level 1 is all about understanding what's going on in your waking life and in your dream life. It can show you the first steps you might take to gain some of that understanding. Understanding what's going on in your dreams while you are sleeping and when you wake up can make the whole experience of dreaming so much more enjoyable.

UNDERSTAND AND REALIZE DREAMS! LEVEL TWO

During the first level, you concentrated on noticing what went on in your dreams. You may have noticed that things didn't always work out the way that you wanted. There may have been many dreams that were missing important elements. Your pictures of the dream may have been blurry or you may have spent a lot of time feeling confused. There were many questions that were asked in the first level to help you better understand what is going on in the dream, so that even if you are a bit confused, you know where to start.

In the second level, you are invited to take a closer look at your dream life, as well as your waking life, so you can start to identify things in your dreams. In some instances, you may remember a dream and think about how confused you were in it. In other dreams, you were able to comprehend what was going on because it related to something you dealt with in your waking life.

The aspiration here is to help you to understand your dreams better. It can be very frustrating to have a dream and never understand what is happening. You may feel confused in the dream, or you may wake up from the dream confused. The steps in this Dream Opportunity can help you understand what is going on in your dreams so you can actually enjoy them.

For the second level in this dream opportunity, you are invited to explore identifying how much you understand in your dream, with the help of a graph. Remember to focus on how clearly you understand what is going on and what it all means to you. Remember to take all your dreams into consideration when determining how clear you are in your dreams.

To begin identifying, start by GRAPHING your clarity. Remember, we are talking about how clearly you understand what is going on and what it means for you. Use the scale given below to rate how much you speak up or express yourself.

Generally, taking all of your dreams into consideration, how clear are you in your dreams?

1. COMPLETELY CONFUSED: Your dream pictures are incoherent and weird – events and feelings have no relationship.
2. UNCLEAR AND INDIRECT: There is much distortion in your dreams, although it does not completely obscure dream pictures or meanings.
3. SOMEWHAT CLEAR AND DIRECT: You have a general idea of what is going on in the dreams, and what your dreams are telling you, even though some elements may be distorted.
4. CLEAR AND DIRECT: Your pictures and the messages you get from your dreams are clear and direct. Dreams seem to make sense, but not completely.
5. COMPLETELY CLEAR AND DIRECT: Your feelings, actions, and the messages you get from the dream are totally clear and direct. There is no distortion. The dream makes sense to you.

Next to your notes about this dream, write the number that corresponds to your general level of clarity in your dream life. GENERAL CLARITY: 1, 2, 3, 4, or 5.

Also next to your notes about this dream, write the number that corresponds to clear you are in this dream. RECENT DREAM CLARITY: 1, 2, 3, 4, or 5.

When you are done taking notes about the dreams that you want to use, write down the number that corresponds to the general level of clarity that happens in your dream. Each dream is going to be slightly different, so you may need to average them or go with each dream on its own. Some dreams will be really unclear in the beginning and you may only have a rating of a one or a two. On the other hand, there may be times when you have clearer dreams and you can rate your dreams with a four or a five.

Sometimes the aspiration here is to get to a five, but it may take some time. Other times, you are comfortable with the level you find – maybe you don't really want to know, or you just don't care. That's okay, too. When you reach a level of five, you may notice that you can look back at your dreams with total clarity. You may be able to answer any questions that you have about your dreams later on, and there aren't any parts that are confusing. This takes some time to accomplish. If you are able to have total clarity in your dreams from the beginning, you are already very fortunate, indeed! Keeping some of the questions in mind and going through Level 1 and Level 2 will help you to get in the flow, to reach that level of total clarity and understanding, simply through considering the clarity of your dreams and doing the exercises that are provided.

Past Questions

At this point, you are going to be invited to start making graphs, so you can see a connection between how much clarity you had at different times in your life and how much clarity is found in your dreams.

1. Using the 1-to-5 scale, on new sheet or page of paper, write the number for your waking activity that best indicates how clear you were during the following periods of your life:

1 - 5 years old
6 - 12 years old
13 - 16 years old
17 - 21 years old
22 - 25 years old
26 - 35 years old
36 - 45 years old
46 - 55 years old
56 - 65 years old
66 - 75 years old
76 years and older

2. Now draw vertical and horizontal lines and numbers to create this graph of your freedom for each period of your life. Place a dot above each age, then connect the dots:

5

4

3

2

1

age   1   6   13   17   22   26   36   46   56   66   76

Your chart will look something like this:

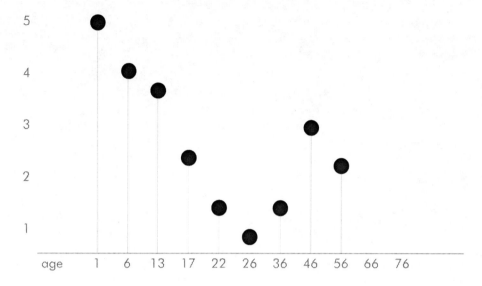

Your completed graph might look something like this after you connect the dots:

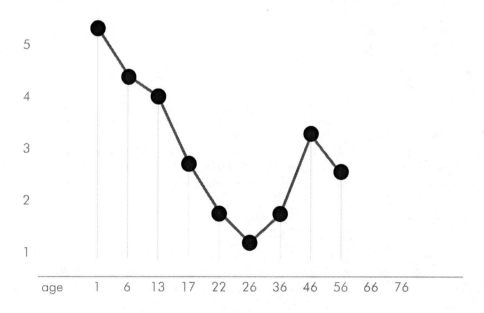

• Now look at the graph. Print it out if you can.
• Notice if your clarity has changed over the years.
• Think about what has happened to you, how you have changed.

You may be able to see how your clarity has changed over the years. Take some time to think about why you have clarity at certain times and why it may have faded at other times throughout your life. Think about what events occurred in your life to increase or reduce your clarity at certain times.

3. Think about how your parents, your friends, and your neighborhood may have determined the level of clarity in your life.

4. Are you satisfied with how clear you are in your waking life?

5. List what kinds of understanding were allowed as you were growing up, and what kinds were frowned upon.

ALLOWED:

a. _____
b. _____
c. _____

FROWNED UPON:

a. _____
b. _____
c. _____

After you invest some time looking at the graph and understanding what's going on with your levels of clarity, it can be helpful to think about the people who may have influenced you through the years. You may find that the people around you, especially those from your background, are able to greatly influence your clarity and how you think about and understand things in your dreams and in your waking life.

You can also consider how satisfied you are with your clarity in your waking life. Do you go through the day feeling confused about the things that are happening? Are you always asking questions and never knowing what is going on? Do you feel that you really understand what is going on each day, or do you feel disappointed with how much you miss out on because you just don't understand what people are talking about around you? If so, it may be time to make some changes.

Dream Opportunity Questions

It's time for some Dream Opportunity Questions! These can help you take a closer look at some of the things that go on in your life and whether you have a helpful amount of clarity or not. The questions for this dream opportunity are:

What would it be like if your life became totally clear to you – if everything made perfect sense and if everything was easy to understand?

What special strengths, gifts, and talents do you have that you don't use?

Whether you realize it or not, this level has asked you to think about a lot of things that most people try their hardest to avoid. Often people spend a lot of time blaming themselves for being a certain way without ever realizing that they were forced to be that way as they grew up. By understanding this Dream Opportunity to the fullest, you may be able to make a big change.

Bonus Exercises

Before you move on to the third level for this dream opportunity, it can be helpful to take some time for a few extra exercises to help you gain more clarity in your dreams. These exercises include:

Past: In any of your dreams, identify and list the ways in the dreams that you felt, acted, and thought that were the way you were as a child.

Present: Try to identify in your most recent dream a single way of talking, feeling, acting, or understanding that is completely yours the way you are now.

Future: Consider how you could have changed or completed your most recent dream:

• How could you have changed how much you spoke up?

• How could you have changed your level of understanding?

• How could you have changed the level of contact you had with other people in the dream?

• How could you have changed the actions you used in the dream?

• How could you have changed your level of feeling?

Identifying how much understanding you have in your waking life and how that connects with how much understanding you have in your dream life may make a big difference. It's not a lot of fun to go through life feeling confused or not understanding what's going on. You may feel like you have no control over what's going on in your life, or you may worry that you won't be able to make decisions because you are short on the information that is needed. But, by working through some of the steps in this section, you can change all that in no time!

UNDERSTAND AND REALIZE DREAMS! LEVEL THREE

It's time to move on to Level 3 of this Dream Opportunity. This level invites you to make changes that you want in your dreams. If you have quite a few dreams that aren't very clear or that leave you feeling confused, now is the time to change this.

1. Are you satisfied with your level of clarity in this dream?

2. What would have to happen in this dream for you to be totally satisfied with your level of clarity about what this dream is telling you?

3. What are you most clear about in this dream?

4. How do you keep yourself confused or unclear?

5. What would you have to do or what would have to happen, for you to be completely clear?

6. Does the level of clarity in this dream work for you or against you?

7. How would you have to change your level of clarity to flow through to a whole new level?

8. Rate the way you make clarity in this dream using the 1 to 5 scale given in Level 2.

Generally, taking all of your dreams into consideration, how clear are you in your dreams?

1. COMPLETELY CONFUSED: Your dream pictures are incoherent and weird – events and feelings have no relationship.
2. UNCLEAR AND INDIRECT: There is much distortion in your dreams, although it does not completely obscure dream pictures or meanings.
3. SOMEWHAT CLEAR AND DIRECT: You have a general idea of what is going on in the dreams, and what your dreams are telling you, even though some elements may be distorted.
4. CLEAR AND DIRECT: Your pictures and the messages you get from your dreams are clear and direct. Dreams seem to make sense, but not completely.
5. COMPLETELY CLEAR AND DIRECT: Your feelings, actions, and the messages you get from the dream are totally clear and direct. There is no distortion. The dream makes sense to you.

What would it be like if you took your level of clarity one level higher?
What would it be like if you took your level of clarity one level lower?

9. What good things might happen if you became as clear as you would like to in your life?

Dream Opportunity Question

For this Dream Opportunity, there is just one question for you to consider:

What would happen to your problems and challenges in life, if you understood clearly what they are telling you?

Finding Your Dream Clarity Word

Write the ten main words you could use to describe what is happening in your dream.

1. _____
2. _____
3. _____
4. _____
5. _____
6. _____
7. _____
8. _____
9. _____
10. _____

Circle five of the words on your list of ten.

From the five circled words, write three on a new page.

1. _____
2. _____
3. _____

Of the three words, circle two.

From the two circled words, write one on a blank page, all by itself. That single word is your Dream Clarity Word. Remember your Dream Clarity Word throughout the day.

Waking Suggestion

Now you will be invited to explore what you are able to do during your waking life, in order to help you to get more clarity in your daily life, which may also lead to more clarity in your dream life. Often, the reason that you aren't able to understand your dreams is because you have trouble understanding what goes on in your day-to-day life. For this waking suggesting, take notice of some of the situations that go on in your waking life. Take notice of any situations that do not seem clear to you, then consider what it might be like if you they were clearer.

1. As you notice situations in which you are not clear, consider what it might be like if you WERE clear, today. As you notice how clear you are, consider what it might be like if you understood a little more... a little less... lessen your clarity a little and then increase it. Be respectful and appropriate. Do not do anything illegal, improper, or harmful during waking life. Try this out all day long, lessen your clarity and understanding a little and then increase it.
2. Before you go on, did you really try out some of those new things? If not, at least notice and identify how you stopped yourself.

Did you get confused?
Less active?
Did you pull back from contact?
Did you restrict your ability to feel good?
Did you speak up less?

Take notice of some of the situations in your waking life where you feel clear, like you understand what is going on around you. During these situations, consider what it would be like if you understood the situation more in some instances, or a little less in other instances. Let your clarity go up and down to see how it all feels. This can help you to realize how to control your own clarity and what you are able to do to create this difference. You can try this out all day long, starting out with increasing your clarity and then decreasing it, until you learn how to gain the control that you are looking for.

Again, please keep in mind that while you are exploring this waking suggestion, it is up to you to do all of this in a respectful and appropriate manner. Never do anything that is harmful, improper, or illegal during your waking life, in order to finish this opportunity. Always be safe and respectful with yourself and others.

Maintaining the Changes

If you have done the exercises in Levels 1, 2, and 3, your dreams have probably begun to change already. Here is a series of questions you can use to maintain the changes:
1. How did you like the level of clarity and understanding you had in this dream?
2. What is the dream trying to tell you about your waking life?
3. What is this dream trying to tell you about your future?
4. How can you change your opportunity so that the present and future circumstances in the story work for you?

If you are not satisfied with your clarity or understanding in your dreams, repeat the exercises in Level 3 on a different day, with a different dream. If you are still not satisfied, repeat them again, on yet another day. You can also return to the exercises in Levels 1 and 2, for greater insight and sensitivity.

Bonus Exercise

Here are a few extra exercises that you can do to help increase your clarity in your dreams. To start, list out all the changes that you want to have in your life for the next year. You can choose what these changes are going to be, whether you want to just change a few little things or you have one big change that you want to make. The list can be as long as you would like, but do try to add on a few different things that you would like to work with.

Once this list is done, make sure to put it somewhere you can see it each day. This will help to remind you of the changes that you want to make, and some of the aspirations you want to reach out for. It is a great way to motivate yourself to keep on growing towards your aspirations, the way growing plants reach for and naturally grow towards sunlight.

Feel free to revise your list as necessary. It can be helpful to review the list each month to make sure that you are sticking with the aspirations you felt for yourself. For example, you may find that you are done with some of the aspirations in a short amount of time, while other times you feel a need to add some or find new ways to make a difference. Reviewing your aspirations on occasion can have a big impact on how motivated you stay for this part of the exercise.

Level 3 is all about helping you to get more clarity and understanding out of the dreams you are dealing with. For some people, this may be fairly easy because they already have clear dreams that they can understand. But for others, this may be a challenge. If you are someone who barely recognizes yourself in your dreams, or you wake up feeling like you are confused or you missed out on something in a dream, then this chapter may be particularly beneficial for you.

IN SUMMARY

Understanding what is going on in your dreams and in your waking life can make things much easier. It is hard to get ahead or talk with anyone if you don't understand what others are telling you. Even your dreams can seem incoherent and hard to understand if you aren't able to understand what's going on in your real life.

In this Dream Opportunity, you were invited to explore adding more clarity to your dreams. You started out by using Level 1 just to notice how clear your dreams are. This can include many things, such as how clear the pictures are in your dreams or even how much confusion you have concerning the events that happened in your dreams. You aren't trying to make any changes at Level 1. Rather, you are taking notice of the way you see your dreams.

Level 2 moved on to identifying some of the clarity that you have. Some of your dreams will have good clarity and some may be confusing. There is a relationship between the clarity you find in your personal life and the clarity you find in your dreams. This section is all about finding this connection so you can make it stronger and so you can understand more of what is going on with your life.

Finally, in the third level, you were invited to make changes. This section has some exercises you can explore, to start adding more clarity to your waking life.

Often the reason that you wake up confused about your dreams is that there are many times in your waking life when you are confused, don't understand what is going on, or don't understand what others are telling you. When you are able to change some of the clarity that you have in your waking life, you are then able to change the clarity you have in your dreams.

Understanding what goes on in your dreams can make a big difference in how much you enjoy your dreams. You may also uncover messages from your dreams. It takes time to gain this confidence and this skill. By following the steps in this Dream Opportunity, you can gain some of the clarity that you are looking for in all your dreams.

EPILOGUE:
HOW TO
BECOME A
DREAMBASSADOR

If some of the topics in this guidebook worked for you and you enjoyed learning about how to deepen, expand, and enhance your experience of dreaming, perhaps you are interested in becoming a *Dreambassador*. This is a great opportunity to be a spokesperson for the value of dreaming – an opportunity that allows you to interact with others, who may need or want help with the different aspects of their dreams, so they can get the most out of their waking and dream lives.

Information about becoming a Dreambassador is available at:
www.Dreamosophy.com

There were five main Dream Opportunities that you explored in this guidebook. Each of them had exercises to help you to deepen, expand, and enhance your experience of your own dreams. If you are like most people, it is not uncommon to find that your dreams lack clarity or that you aren't able to speak up in your dreams. As a Dreambassador, you can help others explore the various steps of this Dreamosophy Approach, whether they are looking to go through just one level or opportunity or whether they're eager to go through all three levels of all five opportunities.

First, you will learn to engage with all your identified dreamers to help them learn how to remember their dreams. If your dreamers are not able to remember their dreams, it is very hard for them to move forward in this approach, because remembering dreams is prerequisite. You can lead them through some of the different steps for remembering their dreams, from getting to bed at a good time, to allowing time to focus on the dreams when they wake up, to writing down notes on dreams.

In the first Dream Opportunity, you will guide others in how to be free in their dreams. This is a huge opportunity that many people still need help with, because they may feel lost and alone when it comes to their dreams. They may let someone else dictate how they behave during the dreams or they may not be able to affect the different things that go on around them, no matter how hard they try. How to Be Free is a great way to help people learn how to deal with and benefit from nightmares.

As a Dreambassador, you can help others gain this freedom by showing them how to recognize their activity level in their dreams and how they can be more free in those dreams. You can help others learn how to make changes in the amount of freedom they have in their waking life, so that freedom can be achieved in the dream life too.

During the second Dream Opportunity, you will learn to engage with your identified dreamers to help them learn to feel good in their dreams. It is usually not very satisfying, when someone wakes up from a dream feeling angry, sad, or upset over something. Many of your dreamers may deal with this in their dreams. The second Dream Opportunity is all about how to feel good in your dreams by controlling your feelings in your dream life and your waking life.

It is not uncommon to find that when someone doesn't feel good in their dreams, it's because they aren't feeling good in their personal lives. This Dream Opportunity allows for a chance to change how happy you feel in your waking life by letting you explore how to control these feelings, whether good or bad, at different times of the day. This control can be very beneficial in your life and may allow you to pick the response that is proper for the case, even in your dreams.

In the third Dream Opportunity, you will learn to engage with your identified dreamers to help them learn to speak up more. This area that is hard for many dreamers, so you may find that you invest the most time on this one. Many people may have dreams where they are just sitting on the sidelines or observing from a disembodied place, watching what happens around them. It is rare that they will speak up or get to choose what happens in the dream, and this can leave them feeling frustrated overall.

Often, the reason that people are not able to speak up in their dreams is that they have trouble speaking up in their waking lives, when they are at work or around other people in their homes or communities. They may go to work and let others make the big decisions. They may stay quiet when they are in social situations, or even at home because they are worried about what others will think about them. This can easily seep into the dreams they have and make it almost impossible for them to have any choices in their dreams.

In this opportunity, you can help your dreamers get through this issue in a safe and effective way. They will first start to notice how they speak up and control what is going on in their dreams as well as in their waking life. They will also invest some time identifying the reasons that they have so much trouble speaking up in their dreams. And finally, you may be able to help your dreamers learn to speak up more in their personal lives, whether this means sharing more when they are at work, making new friends, or doing other things to help them express themselves more on a regular basis.

Through the fourth Dream Opportunity you will learn to engage with your identified dreamers to help them learn to make some friends in their dreams. This can be a big deal for people who may feel that they are just spending their time watching a show while dreaming, rather than focusing on making friends. It is possible to interact and make friendships with others who are in your dreams, and you can help your dreamers learn how to do this.

In this Dream Opportunity, you can help your dreamers learn to make some new friendships in their personal lives as well as in their dream lives. Sometimes, the reason your dreamers are on the sidelines when it comes to making new friends in their dreams is that they are not having much luck making friends in their waking lives. As the Dreambassador, you can help your dreamers to notice how they make connections in their dreams, as well as give them the steps to help them make more friendships in their waking life.

And finally, in the fifth Dream Opportunity you will learn to engage with your identified dreamers to help them learn to understand and realize their fondest dreams. There are many times when people will wake up from a dream feeling like they missed out on something important, or that they were not able to understand something that went on. In other instances, they may not have been able to see themselves or the pictures or meaning in the dream as clearly as they would like. Often, this confusion results from confusion found in their personal, waking life.

Changing the understandings that people have in their personal lives about different circumstances they might deal with can help them gain more understanding of their dreams, and vice versa. In this Dream Opportunity, you are responsible for helping your dreamers realize how much more they can understand of what is going on in their personal and dream life with the help of the exercises in this guidebook.

These are the five Dream Opportunities that you can explore with your dreamers. Sometimes, you can explore on all of them with your dreamers, to help them to gain a full understanding of their dreams. It is easy to get caught up in a daily life where it feels like there is no control, but with the help of the exercises in each of the Dream Opportunities, your dreamers can learn to make changes to their dreams.

Ideally, you will go through these different Dream Opportunities to help you learn how each one works, and then use the things that you learned to help your dreamers get into a nourishing flow, in their dream lives and their waking lives. Each of the Dream Opportunities will have the same basic setup, making them easy for you to explore. Each opportunity begins with noticing – noticing what is going on in the dreams and how dreamers react in different situations. The first level of each opportunity is not about making things change; it is about noticing what is going on.

Then, each Dream Opportunity moves on to helping your dreamers identify what is going on in their dreams and make connections with what they are doing in their waking life. This part includes a rating system and some graphing so that they can see how it all comes together in a visual format.

The third level of your Dream Opportunities is all about change and transformation. It is about seeing how people behave in their waking life and helping them learn how to make gentle changes, while they are awake, that influence how they dream. When people are able to affect how they feel, how they speak up, how they make friends, and how they understand and realize dreams, they may be better able to find overall satisfaction in life. That can be one of the best things about this whole process – that with a bit of careful attention to dream life, it is easy to make some of the changes that people want to have happen!

When you engage with your dreamers, it is important to make a plan that is unique to them. Some people may only benefit from attending to a few of the Dream Opportunities and others may benefit more from all of them. In addition, there are times when a dreamer may be able to get through each level in less than a week, other dreamers who will benefit more from investing a few weeks on each level, and still others who may benefit from going back through the levels a few times before it all fits together. There is no way to fall behind or do poorly – this is THEIR process. They will benefit most by going at the speed that is right for them. Engage with your dreamers to help them feel comfortable and realize that they are making great progress simply by attending to their dream life.

Becoming a Dreambassador can be a great experience. It allows you to help others who may be having issues with their dreams, whether they are in a position to benefit from a few of the Dream Opportunities or from all of them. Getting to talk about and learn about all of this with your dreamers can make a big difference in the quality of dreams that everyone experiences.

CONCLUSION

The Dreamosophy approach is one that can work for many different people, in very diverse ways. It has been set up to make transforming your dreams easier than ever before. Whether you are looking to change your dreams all on your own or you want to become a Dreambassador and help others, there can be great joy in being able to deepen, expand, and enhance the ways you experience your dream life.

In this guidebook, you were introduced to the five Dream Opportunities that can help you to make some profound changes in your dreams and even in your waking life – how to be free in your dreams, how to feel good in your dreams, how to speak up in your dreams, how to make friends in your dreams, and how to understand and realize your fondest dreams.

When all these Dream Opportunities come together, and you learn from the exercises that come with them, you may see some profound changes in your dreams. It is important that you consider each level of each Dream Opportunity sincerely, to help you see these changes. Sometimes, you may be able to zip through one of the opportunities without too much time or attention, but other times, you may benefit from going through an opportunity a few times, to get the results that you prefer. Everyone can go at their own pace, to see some results. So have fun and explore what you have learned from these opportunities!

ABOUT THE
AUTHOR

PAUL SHELDON

For Paul Sheldon, a childhood filled with dancing, singing, gardening and open-hearted exploring of various aspects of consciousness and spiritual experience flowed smoothly into an adulthood of consulting and advising, tree planting, and social activism for institutional transformation, through helping people, organizations, and communities realize their fondest dreams. Paul is fascinated by all kinds of wisdom, especially as expressed through the use of water-based metaphors – a fascination which emerged from explorations of lucid dreaming.

As a private Development Consultant, Paul Sheldon specializes in helping clients realize their fondest dreams. To do this, he works with dreams – both the dreams recalled from sleep, as well as all kinds of visualization, imagination, creativity, goal setting, and creative approaches to the realization of individual and collective dreams. He also works with clients to increase their access to the resources needed to realize their dreams, through real estate, organizational development, green jobs development, energy efficiency planning, implementing sustainability, staff training, the greening of jails, prisons, and other correctional institutions, and the co-creation of a regenerative world – Paul believes strongly that it is too late just to do no harm – we must participate actively in the healing of each other and the world in which we live – what in Hebrew is described as "Tikkun Olam" – the healing of the world. He consults widely for businesses, governments, non-profit groups, and philanthropists. Paul has written reports on Coal Plants in Transition—Economic and Energy Alternatives to coal, the REEL in Alaska Roadmap to energy efficiency in the Railbelt Region around Anchorage, Alaska, and the viability of solar power on the Navajo Nation, as well as scholarly articles on the Helix of Sustainable Management, the Integrated Bottom Line, and greening prisons. He is the primary author of the National Institute of Justice Greening Corrections Technology Guidebook, as well as the American Correctional Association's policy and standard on sustainability-oriented and environmentally responsible practices in corrections. Paul finds prisons and jails to be a wonderful metaphor for being imprisoned in the human condition – a condition from which dreaming can be an important escape. In addition to his role as Founder of Dreamosophy.com, Paul serves as Manager Member of JLMJ, LLC, a small, private investment group, as Development Consultant for the Laura X Institute (www.LauraXinstitute.org), as Development Director and member of the board of directors of Planting Justice (www.PlantingJustice.org) – an Oakland-based charity dedicated to food justice, economic justice, and regenerative local food systems – and has served as a Senior Advisor to Natural Capitalism Solutions (www.natcapsolutions.org), as Underwriting Consultant to California's State Workers' Compensation Insurance Fund, and has worked closely with his older sister, Hunter Lovins, co-teaching "Principles of Sustainable Business Management," "Implementing Sustainable Business Practices," and "Effective Management, Communication and Action" (with Bob Dunham), at Presidio Graduate School, the first fully accredited M.B.A. program in Sustainable Management (www.presidio.edu). Paul and Hunter also helped to start the Los Angeles-based TreePeople (www.Treepeople.org) and the Rocky Mountain Institute (www.rmi.org). His clients have included the U.S. Department of State, U.S. EPA, Natural Resources Canada, Alaska Conservation Association, Chugach Electric Association, California Energy Commission, California Public Utilities Commission, General Motors, Bank of America, Muzak, Suzuki Motors, and many cities and local organizations. Paul also has extensive business experience in publishing, wholesale and retail travel, hospitality, real estate, personnel, auditing, and insurance industries, is an active member of the American Correctional Association and the American Jail Association, and is a former member of the Vocational Advisory Board for Soledad State Prison, former member of the Humboldt County Workforce Investment Board, former owner of a local personnel/staffing service, and an advisor to the U.S. Department of State.

Paul holds B.A. and M.A. degrees in Human Development, from Pacific Oaks College, in Pasadena, California and a lifetime college teaching credential in Business and Industrial Management, is a certified business analyst, an Honorary Member, Rocky Mountain Association of Energy Engineers, and a founding member of the Sustainability Committee of the American Correctional Association. Paul lives with his wife, in Ashland, Oregon, and is an avid folk dancer, gardener, amateur botanist, and follower of the Sant Mat yoga tradition.

DREAMOSOPHY
DREAM
JOURNAL

DREAMOSOPHY DREAMSTREAM JOURNAL

DREAM TITLE:
DATE:
LOCATION:
DREAM STORY:

REMEMBERING DREAMS PRACTICE – DREAM #1

DREAM TITLE:
DATE:
LOCATION:
DREAM STORY:

REMEMBERING DREAMS PRACTICE – DREAM #2

DREAM TITLE:
DATE:
LOCATION:
DREAM STORY:

REMEMBERING DREAMS PRACTICE – DREAM #3

DREAM TITLE:
DATE:
LOCATION:
DREAM STORY:

HOW TO BE FREE! LEVEL ONE

DREAM TITLE:
DATE:
LOCATION:
DREAM STORY:

HOW TO BE FREE! LEVEL TWO

DREAM TITLE:
DATE:
LOCATION:
DREAM STORY:

HOW TO BE FREE! LEVEL THREE

DREAM TITLE:
DATE:
LOCATION:
DREAM STORY:

HOW TO FEEL GOOD! LEVEL ONE

DREAM TITLE:
DATE:
LOCATION:
DREAM STORY:

HOW TO FEEL GOOD! LEVEL TWO

DREAM TITLE:
DATE:
LOCATION:
DREAM STORY:

HOW TO FEEL GOOD! LEVEL THREE

DREAM TITLE:
DATE:
LOCATION:
DREAM STORY:

HOW TO SPEAK UP! LEVEL ONE

DREAM TITLE:
DATE:
LOCATION:
DREAM STORY:

HOW TO SPEAK UP! LEVEL TWO

DREAM TITLE:
DATE:
LOCATION:
DREAM STORY:

HOW TO SPEAK UP! LEVEL THREE

DREAM TITLE:
DATE:
LOCATION:
DREAM STORY:

HOW TO MAKE FRIENDS! LEVEL ONE

DREAM TITLE:
DATE:
LOCATION:
DREAM STORY:

HOW TO MAKE FRIENDS! LEVEL TWO

DREAM TITLE:
DATE:
LOCATION:
DREAM STORY:

HOW TO MAKE FRIENDS! LEVEL THREE

DREAM TITLE:
DATE:
LOCATION:
DREAM STORY:

HOW TO UNDERSTAND AND REALIZE! LEVEL ONE

DREAM TITLE:
DATE:
LOCATION:
DREAM STORY:

HOW TO UNDERSTAND AND REALIZE! LEVEL TWO

DREAM TITLE:
DATE:
LOCATION:
DREAM STORY:

HOW TO UNDERSTAND AND REALIZE! LEVEL THREE

DREAM TITLE:
DATE:
LOCATION:
DREAM STORY:

NOTES:

NOTES:

CPSIA information can be obtained
at www.ICGtesting.com
Printed in the USA
FSOW02n1059010817
37069FS